Achieving Best Practice
Shaping Professionals
for Success

GW00468031

Achieving Best Practice
Shaping Professionals
for Success

by

Fiona Westwood

THE McGRAW-HILL COMPANIES

London · Burr Ridge IL · New York · St Louis · San Francisco · Auckland
Bogotá · Caracas · Lisbon · Madrid · Mexico · Milan · Montreal
New Delhi · Panama · Paris · San Juan · São Paulo
Singapore · Sydney · Tokyo · Toronto

Published by
McGraw-Hill Publishing Company
SHOPPENHANGERS ROAD, MAIDENHEAD, BERKSHIRE SL6 2QL, ENGLAND
Telephone +44 (0) 1628 502500
Fax: +44 (0) 1628 770224   Web site: http://www.mcgraw-hill.co.uk

---

British Library Cataloguing in Publication Data
A catalogue record for this book is available from the British Library

ISBN 0 07 709749 1

Library of Congress Cataloging-in-Publication Data
A catalogue record for this book has been requested

Sponsoring Editor   Elizabeth Robinson
Produced by   Steven Gardiner Ltd
Cover by   Simon Levy

Authors website: www.westwood-associates.com

McGraw-Hill

A Division of The McGraw·Hill Companies

1 2 3 4 5 CUP 4 3 2 1 0
Printed and bound in Great Britain at the University Press, Cambridge

Contents

Contents

Contents

Preface

This book is written by a professional for professionals.

It has stemmed from my own experiences and frustrations. In the late 1980s, I had made it to equity partner in one of the larger law practices in Scotland. As part of its management team, I was well aware of the particular problems facing professional service firms. Speaking with colleagues and friends, I realised that my firm was not alone. All of the professions – including law, accountancy, architecture, medicine and teaching – seemed to be experiencing drastic reductions in lifestyles and quality of living. Job satisfaction had become a thing of the past, with incomes and relationships under severe pressure. Common themes included the erosion of traditional areas of fee income, the impact of technology and increasing "consumerism" from clients.

Professionals are intelligent people, committed to continuous training and development. Why was this happening to us? What was stopping us from responding in a positive way to these challenges? How could we adapt? What lessons could we learn from other organisations?

Looking for help in traditional management books, I found them cumbersome and written in a language more suited to large corporations rather than the professions. They talked about strategy, production and marketing in such a way as made little sense to the informality of partnerships and client services. Yet, the more I became involved in the challenges of running a professional firm, the more convinced I was that solutions did exist. Yes, the market place was changing but the core values of professionalism should not be compromised. Yes, clients were demanding more of their professionals, but that had to be good news for organisations committed to high-quality services.

I worked alongside my partners, seeking solutions to these problems. I worked with my commercial clients observing how they developed strategies and implemented change. I served on the Steering Group of an Enterprise Centre dedicated to support business start-up and growth and saw it develop into a European model of best practice. I became UK Chair of a multidiscipline network of construction professionals and learned the strengths of these professions and their similarities. And for the past 6 years, I have concentrated on helping organisations grow and develop – to build on the strengths of their firms and their clients. Ten years on, I know success is possible. There are examples of

Preface

professional organisations who have succeeded in tackling these challenges without compromising their professionalism.

This book is what I needed all those years ago. It closes the gap that exists between the theory and practice. Based on qualitative research and experience of successful professional firms across the UK, the content reflects the needs of professionals trying to manage themselves and their organisations. It offers a Model which appreciates their problems and puts them into context. It provides a holistic view of the firm, looks at its internal workings and external focus. Its segments encompass leadership and management, strategy and processes. They provide practical techniques and solutions. They build into a complete circle of knowledge and understanding of management and its application, which provides the ability to change, vital in today's environment. Over and above, it is written by a professional who cares about the professions – who believes that they have a future and deserve success.

Fiona Westwood
April 2000

Acknowledgements

This book is a reflection of working in partnership with people we trust and respect. I value the help I receive from these relationships. These include all of the professionals and their organisations involved in the research into the Model for Success, as well as my clients who continue to allow me to develop my skills and expertise.

In addition, there are a number of associates and close friends who give me their time and energy at whatever hour of the day or night I demand it! In particular, I want to thank:

- Diane Irvine for her positive reinforcement and support (including bringing light relief and refreshments when required);
- Lorna McEachan for her empathy and practical advice (as well as encouraging me out into the fresh air occasionally); and
- Martyn Robertson for his vision and willingness to play devil's advocate whenever I needed to be challenged!

Over and above all, I want to thank my young people, Caroline and Henry, for putting up with my preoccupation (they may well describe it as obsession!) with this book, even to the extent of allowing me to take my laptop on holiday.

About the author

Fiona Westwood graduated LLB (Hons) from Glasgow University in 1974 and became an enrolled solicitor with the Law Society of Scotland in 1976.

During her professional career as a solicitor, which spanned 20 years, she had a wide and general experience of client work. This ranged from running a branch specialising in legal aid through to establishing and managing a large commercial-property department. In 1987, she was headhunted to help manage an ambitious amalgamation of three long established firms, where she had particular responsibility for business development of the new firm.

She worked in private practice in Scotland until setting up her own management consultancy in 1994. She currently works with a wide range of professional and commercial clients. Recent commercial clients have included BAE Systems and Scottish Power. Public-sector clients include the Ministry of Defence, the Scottish Executive and a wide range of business-support agencies.

She has served on the Steering Group and was Vice-chair of the board of Wellpark Enterprise Centre which has become a European model of best practice in the field of business start-up and growth support.

Within the professional sector, clients include a wide range of private-practice firms from all professional disciplines, private hospitals and hospital trusts, and higher and further-education establishments.

In 1994–5 she held the position of UK Chair of Women in Property, a multidiscipline network for professionals working in the property and construction sector.

More information about the author and her firm can be obtained from her website: www.westwood-associates.com

1. Introduction

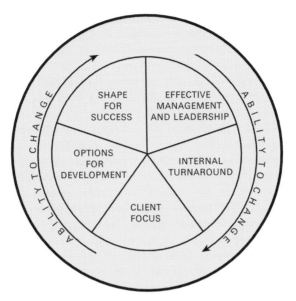

THE MODEL FOR SUCCESS

1.1 Professionals are under pressure

Professionals are under pressure! They are facing change at a rate never before experienced by them. Regardless of whether they work in private practice or in commercial or not-for-profit organisations, they are being asked to change the way that they deliver their services.

Within my own professional career, which started in 1974, I have seen long-established practices wither and die, income levels drop alarmingly and workloads increase drastically. In the 1980s, the firm I worked with had an established and loyal client base that paid us without question and left us to get on with the work. Good connections referred us quality work with fees rendered every month without apparent effort or difficulty. Partners enjoyed a pleasant lifestyle and were active in the local community. They had time for sport, leisure activities and holidays, secure in the knowledge that a stable and dedicated staff could be depended on to keep the business ticking over.

All of this has now gone. Client loyalty is a thing of the past with clients often shopping around for the best deal, and increasingly litigious if their professional fails to deliver what they want. Patients no longer accept the advice of their doctor without question. Clients are better informed and have many sources of information. Professionals are increasingly on the receiving end of bad publicity with stories of "fat cats", inflated earnings and abuse of their powers. Professional expertise is becoming more complex with constant changes in legislation, regulations and technology. Doing a quality job is now the minimum requirement, with professionals expected to add value and not hide behind a basic professional service.

All professionals are being asked to be more accountable, either to outside bodies and/or for budgets and levels of performance. Their professional bodies, who impose high duties of care, significantly influence professionals. All of this can cause conflict between professional and "commercial" values.

For professional firms, the market has become more competitive with a resulting downward effect on fees, which has put pressure on cash flow and profitability. Relationships between partners have become strained with a lack of trust and mutual support developing. People seem to be working harder and harder for less return. They complain of a lack of job satisfaction, of an unacceptable standard of living, and of increasing health problems.

For professionals working in commercial or not-for-profit organisations, financial budgets appear to be driving decisions. Professionals are being asked to agree performance levels, and work within targets and constraints. Commercial managers often describe professionals as "devil's advocates", blocking decisions and putting obstacles in their way.

1.2 What is the effect?

The effect of this is serious, both in the short and long term. As the world becomes more complex, this requires ever-increasing investment in technology, training and communications. As a result, all professionals feel under pressure to develop new skills and adapt their traditional approach to service delivery. They are having to cope with an increased emphasis on business, budgets and management.

Within private practice, partners are working long hours in an attempt to sustain income levels. They have neither the time nor energy to think creatively, to develop new business connections or new skills. They are reluctant to share client work with others, fearing that they will be forced out of the firm if they appear not to be needed. This results in partners not asking for help, either when they are overloaded or in an area outwith their expertise. This can have drastic effects on client services and complaints.

Within firms, tensions are appearing amongst relationships. Trading as partnerships demands absolute trust between the partners. When this breaks down, as a result of declining profits and increasing workloads, a blame culture often develops. This further deprives the firm of the ability to talk issues through or work together to agree the future of the firm. Resources already under pressure become increasingly an issue, with senior partners looking to retirement and their pensions, and junior partners wanting to invest in new technology.

Professionals working in the public or private sectors describe similar tensions. They are often in a conflicted position as they try to point out professional issues to managers who are reluctant to listen to them. Decisions seem to be based on external drivers rather than service quality. They feel that they have to juggle the demands of their organisations with their professional values. They may have to spend time in meetings about budgets rather than on patient, student or client care.

The end result of this is that professionals need help. Their problems are particular and complex. They need to be able to balance the needs of their clients, their organisations and themselves. Professional partnerships have additional difficulties imposed by their structure, where force of personality can have a powerful influence.

1.3 Why this book helps

Traditional management techniques need to be put into this professional context. This book does just that. It is designed to give practical and pragmatic advice with Key-Action Points summarised at the end of each chapter. Examples are given of particular professional problems. Tools and techniques are developed to provide solutions and put them into practice.

During the late 1980s and early 1990s, I was part of the management team in a large law firm. I had responsibility for developing a specialist client-service department from scratch, as well as business development for the firm as a whole. We were trying to cope with the issues of an ambitious growth strategy at a time when the property market was depressed. Our strategy, based on market expansion by way of amalgamation, had brought with it a wide range of client, resource and "people" problems.

Looking for help in the existing management books, I found that many were too cumbersome for a busy professional. I had neither the time nor the inclination to wade through much of what is irrelevant to the particular needs of my situation. Some were simplistic, asking me to swallow what was written on trust and apply it without question. I could find little that was directly relevant to the problems I faced. None of this was palatable to a professional who had been trained to analyse information, test its validity and question assumptions! I was therefore forced to interpret the theory and put it into the context of my own firm. As a result, I became more interested in management than the law, and since 1994, have worked exclusively with commercial and professional organisations helping them and the people within them to develop.

This book is a reflection of my own experiences and those of my clients. It is written primarily for those professionals either working in or directly with professional firms. As a result, they are struggling with the "unmanageability" of partnerships – trying to persuade partners to work together, improve profits yet maintain a quality professional service, attract and retain good clients and staff. Many professions think that their problems are unique, but these issues are common to the whole professional sector, whether it be accounting, legal, surveying, architecture, general medical practice or dentistry.

In addition, this book is for people who work with professionals in any context, which includes commercial organisations as well as not-for-profit situations, such as hospitals, universities and colleges. Putting professionals into a traditional management structure can cause "manageability" problems. Current pressures on these types of organisation include the need to become more customer focused and commercial. Professionals often see this as a direct challenge to their values and can become at best mischievous and at worst, disruptive.

Finally, this book is aimed at all organisations of the future. It is now accepted theory in Western economies that competitive advantage will only come from becoming knowledge based. The West is becoming less able to compete with developing countries on production and labour costs. To respond to this, Western economies need to become innovators with fast response times and flexible delivery mechanisms. They need to develop new ways of working. The proposed role models for these new workers are professionals, on the premis that they already are knowledge workers. Yet, as indicated above, professionals are not easy to manage and we need to understand them before attempting to do so. This book is therefore designed to help those forward-looking organisations that are taking up the challenge and wish to succeed in the knowledge economy.

1.4 Professional versus commercial

Many professionals feel that there is a dichotomy between being both professional and commercial. They are uncomfortable with what they see as too much emphasis on the financial aspects of running the business at the expense of the quality of client services. This is based on the premiss that business people are in some way unethical, selling the public products and services which they either do not want or cannot afford. By comparison, professionals look after the best interests of their clients, without consideration of the profit element and defend the clients' position regardless of their own self-interests. Part of this dichotomy also stems from a general unhappiness about the need to talk about money, as many professionals are uncomfortable about putting a price on what they do.

In my view, there is and should be no dichotomy between being both commercial and professional. Good business people also excel at customer service, work long hours and take considerable risks to ensure the viability of their products and services. Similarly, those tasked with managing professional firms want the ultimate in high-quality client services to achieve and maintain competitive advantage. Few commercial organisations would ask their professionals to behave unprofessionally. Quite apart from the tensions that would create within the organisation, its commercial future would be damaged. Its success will be based on the quality of its services and the dedication of its team of people.

For example, no commercially minded chief executive of a private hospital would ask his or her professional team to compromise professional services. Such an approach would result in both commercial and professional suicide with, at best, poor patient care and bad publicity and, at worst, professional indemnity claims. Good professionals would leave and its poor reputation and image would affect the recruitment of replacements.

Being commercial is nothing more than making sure that the organisation delivers to its maximum potential. For profit-making businesses, this includes financial rewards and returns, current and future investment and targets. For not-for-profit organisations, the targets may be softer, such as levels of achievement gained by students or patients treated. As a result, all fall within the definition of commercial.

1.5 Why are professional firms so difficult to manage?

AGREE!

First of all, partnerships are not an easy structure to manage. For example, planning and decision making usually requires consensus of most, if not all, of the partners. Even where management responsibility has been devolved to one or a number of people, individual partners can still block implementation. Many partners' meetings result in agreement in principle to introduce a different way of working, which will not be implemented in practice by the very partners who agreed to it. Limiting their access to information or imposing sanctions is impossible where partners also happen to own the business!

Another management issue stems from the nature of professionals. By virtue of their background and training, they tend to be articulate, enjoying analysis and debate. They are therefore unlikely to do as they are told, and can become mischievous and difficult if they feel that their professionalism is being threatened. This theme will be developed in later chapters, but one of the main ways to manage professionals is through the identification and delivery of their values.

1.6 The importance of values

The importance of values forms a key element of this book. All professionals and professions place a great deal of emphasis on them, and, as a result, they profoundly affect their behaviours. This will be explained in more detail in Chapter 3. Values can be defined as the basic foundation of what people believe – these principles which, if challenged or threatened, people will fight to defend.

To illustrate their importance, we can all cite examples of leaving an organisation when our values were not being delivered. This did not mean that the organisation was unethical. It simply meant that our values were not the same as the other people working there. This theme is significant as it provides useful information for firms recruiting new personnel. Asking people to describe what is important to them will provide an indication of their values and what drives them.

Values are therefore of considerable importance when we come to consider strategy and management in later chapters. We will develop tools which help us identify, match and deliver these values. They will help us shape our organisations – now and in the future.

1.7 Does shape and size matter?

The shape of organisations is also important. Not only does the structure affect the way people behave, it also influences communications, responsibilities and attitude. A "good structure" can facilitate success, a "poor structure" can cause a great deal of wastage and confusion.

Trading structures open to professional firms are (at the time of writing) still subject to constraints imposed by legislation and/or their professional bodies. For example, doctors cannot trade as limited companies. Solicitors in Scotland cannot share profits with anyone who is not a solicitor enrolled with the Law Society of Scotland. Multidiscipline partnerships (MDPs) continue to be discussed by the professional bodies, with some already allowed, subject to certain requirements. Most professions continue to trade as partnerships, although other options are open to them. Legislation is expected soon to allow limited-liability partnerships.

It seems accepted that MDPs will happen later rather than sooner. Individual professional bodies have put considerable effort into this debate in recent years. They have identified the issues which would need to be addressed, such as conflict of interest and protection for clients. They have also developed a number of models or options. All of this continues to require adjustment and negotiation between the affected parties. However, a number of the larger professional firms have already altered their operational style to work within these restrictions, rather than wait until the matter has been formalised. This has resulted in complicated accounting, with "sister" firms being set up in different disciplines or jurisdictions. This is setting a market trend which some of the smaller firms will find difficult to follow. In my opinion, some of the professions are being unduly hampered by these restrictions and there is a need for the professional bodies to make progress in this area.

Professional firms operate in a variety of structures. A few have become limited companies or partly limited companies, often hiving off the higher risk work. Others prefer to trade as partnerships, based on the flexibility that it allows. Others describe the importance of trust which is essential in an unlimited-liability situation. They argue that partnership encourages "the commitment that comes from being an owner of the business". Others ascribe other values to partnership, such as "collegiate support – the ability to share problems and ideas". All have developed a shape which suits them and their values.

There is a growing perception today that size matters! It is true that the larger organisations and practices often appear to have an increased resource base. They may, for example, be able to employ in-house marketing and financial expertise and invest more heavily in technology. Whilst this provides the potential for growth within these firms, they can also be handicapped by their increased size when it comes to decision making and implementation. They may not be able to adapt and respond as quickly as smaller firms.

The issue of effective management of resources will be looked at in more detail in Chapter 4. The option of using amalgamation and joint ventures as a way of increasing the size of the firm will also be considered. Each has advantages and disadvantages. In general terms, firms should not seek to increase their size alone. This should not be the main driver. Rather they should have identified a direction that they wish to take which increasing the size of the firm will help to support.

One theme will run through all our discussions. Whatever shape is chosen, it is essential that it is fluid enough to achieve change whilst, at the same time, allowing the organisation to deliver quality client services.

1.8 Coping with change

At the beginning of this chapter it was pointed out that the professions are experiencing change at an alarming rate. The particular drivers behind that will be looked at in the next and later chapters, but in general terms the market place is changing and all organisations are being forced to respond.

Triggers for change can be both positive and negative. They can result from a need to manage growth, a drive for continuous improvement, the need to respond to new technology and/or a shift in the market place. They can result from changes in the supply of people and/or other resources. They can also come about as a result of the loss of key people and/or clients, by changes in funding, by poor profitability and service.

Even where the impetus for change comes as the result of positive reasons, people find it hard to respond. This is partly because we may need to stop doing things that we are good at and learn new skills. Few people like to move out of their "comfort zone". An inappropriate structure and a negative culture can compound difficulties. People, regardless of their position in an organisation, have a powerful influence on what succeeds and what fails.

Professional firms are no different when it comes to welcoming changes in the way that they operate. Many are long established serving a wide range of clients. They will have inherited a structure, staff and behaviours, adopting a "family" orientation to the appointment of new partners and the way that they operate. In the past, they were protected from the market place and its pressures. Partnership decision making is cumbersome and firms often have limited management experience. This restricts their ability to respond and adapt and makes change difficult to achieve.

Partners will often say with pride that their firm was set up in the 1870s. Whilst business research indicates that young firms are more likely to fail, many professional firms have become "too old". This results in entrenched behaviours and work practices and a head-in-the-sand approach to problems. Partners complain that professional life "isn't what is used to be". Many hope that if they ignore any pressure to change long enough, they will be able to retire before it directly affects them or their firms!

As a result, change is not easy to manage. Many organisations struggle with change management, spending a lot of time and energy trying to implement new ways of working. Most large organisations accept that to implement a change-culture programme will take a minimum of 5 years. However, it is important to be able to change now and keep changing. Professionals and their organisations need to develop this ability. They need to begin to understand the market place and take control of it. They need to be able to adjust and respond to it. Key skills include clear leadership, good communications, and a willingness to adapt and learn.

1.9 The development of the Model for Success

The book presents a Model which will allow such organisations to change and become successful. Working in and with professional partnerships, I was aware that some firms were successful where others were not. Why was this the case? What made them different? The market pressures were the same, so why were they able to respond and respond well? I wanted to identify what made them able to change and what allowed them to continue to do so.

I investigated over sixty professional firms across the UK in more detail. These included surveyors, architects, civil engineers, lawyers, doctors and accountants. Some were small, others large. A few had incorporated, most were still partnerships. Some were long established, some recently. I looked at a range of features – size, structure, management style, client development, use of technology, amalgamations, formal alliances, diversification – in an attempt to establish what they did well and why they were different.

Were they more successful if they became limited companies? Was partnership as a trading structure a constraint to growth? Certainly, many professionals advise their clients against selecting this option. Was age of the firm important? Were new firms more successful than long established ones? Did amalgamations provide a quick way to grow? Was investment in technology rewarded with increased profitability? Had they changed their shape in recent years? Did they have a formal management structure?

As a result, I was able to identify what made these professional firms successful. First and foremost, these firms were able to change. They may have had to take some hard decisions to allow them to do that, but all of them had learned to move forward. In particular, they:

- had accepted that they needed to be commercially aware;
- had reviewed their client services and the way that these were delivered;
- were aware of their strengths and played to them;

- were aware of their weaknesses and had tackled them through investment in technology and/or training;
- managed their resources effectively and were able, if needed, to call on additional resources through direct funding or through joint ventures;
- had managers and leaders who were trusted and respected within the organisation, and were well regarded within the business community;
- managed their client base well with close and regular contact maintained; and
- most importantly, they were able to carry through any initiatives or changes they decided to implement.

In addition, I found that partnership as a trading structure had a direct influence on the way that firms operated. Used well, it allowed the very flexibility and speed of response that the modern market place demanded. Used badly, however, it inhibited decision making, blocked creativity and did a great deal of damage to client services and the way that people operated.

Another important issue that developed from the initial research was that professionals appear to be strongly influenced by their values, which had a direct effect on their behaviour. Was this particular to professionals in professional firms, or was it common to professionals in general? I developed some examples and tested them on a range of professionals working in both the commercial and not-for-profit sector. I also looked at the Model to see whether it was relevant to their situations. I found that professional values and independence continued to have key prominence and that the Model for Success was applicable to all organisations involving professionals.

Professionals behave the same in all organisations in that:

- their professionalism is very important to them;
- they respond to people that they trust and respect;
- they resist being told what to do;
- they will be the judge of their own competence; and
- they resent any attempts to impose policies and procedures on them. *TRUE*

Within commercial and not-for-profit organisations, particular difficulties can arise when the advice given by professionals conflicts with the aims or plans of senior managers. Whenever possible, professionals will seek ways of balancing these demands. On the occasions when the advice is not adopted, most professionals will resign rather than compromise their values.

1.10 How do we use it?

Since its inception, the Model for Success has been adjusted and refined. It is now based on the experiences of many professional and commercial organisations. Within the confines of client confidentiality, these will be used as illustrative examples throughout the book.

The Model for Success is based on the concept of a wheel with five segments. It encourages organisations to:

- establish effective management and leadership;
- use their resources well;
- become client focused;
- identify and develop options for the future; and
- adjust the shape of the organisation to support all of this.

Each segment will be developed in more detail in later chapters, with practical tools to help to put them into practice. Individual samples and examples will also be given based on the successes of a range of professions.

Each segment is important, but the Model itself is designed to be holistic. The segments build into a complete wheel. The picture of the wheel has been chosen with care, because it represents rotation and movement. Each segment has to be in place to allow the wheel to turn (i.e. to change). By working through all five, organisations develop their skills and their resource base. The process itself is important as it provides the foundation for success. By tackling each section, people learn to work together – to talk about difficult issues and address areas which in the past have been avoided.

To allow organisations to position themselves, there are a series of questions at pages 157–164 to encourage them to identify how well they are currently doing. These questions are broken down to match the segment headings. If they can answer yes to all of the questions, then they will be able to achieve that segment and move on to the next. If they cannot, then the chapter will allow them to identify key actions or priorities.

Given my earlier comments about the need for professions to analyse and develop ideas for themselves, I will not attempt to offer prescriptive solutions! Rather I will provide practical concepts for firms to apply to their own situation. From the outset, I must emphasise that there is no right answer to improving the performance of professionals, just as there is no right school for all children – there is only the right school for the particular child and his or her particular needs. The strength of professionals and their organisations lies in the variety of styles and approaches that are possible. It is vital therefore that each organisation and the individuals working within it establishes their own solution.

The earlier segments of the Model offer fundamental concepts to enable organisations to manage themselves better. We will work through the process of establishing leadership and trust as well as acquiring basic information about the organisation's strengths and weaknesses. Later segments build on this, allowing organisations to actively change the way that people work to develop innovative solutions to future client delivery. In addition, as people work through and complete each segment, the organisation will develop the key for continued growth and success – the ability to change and keep changing.

CONCLUSIONS

The market place is changing, forcing all organisations to adapt and respond. This is putting pressure on everyone, as they have to come to terms with constant change. Professionals have additional problems as they seek to balance the demands of their professionalism with the needs of their organisations.

Professional organisations are difficult to manage because of their structure and inherent behaviours. Values are important to them and influence their shape and style of approach. Professionals need to be able to respond and adapt their service delivery. They also need to be able to balance workloads and income levels. As a result, they have to address fundamental issues around management of their organisations to develop ways of building resources for the future. The Model for Success has been developed from research into and direct observation of professionals and their organisations. It contains five key elements which when combined, create the ability to change which is vital for success today and in the future.

 ## *KEY ACTION POINTS*

≫ Accept that change is unavoidable

≫ Accept that people are currently working under pressure

≫ Respond to change in a positive way

≫ Identify and take control of problems

≫ Always remember that success is possible

2. Setting the Scene

THE MODEL FOR SUCCESS

2.1 Introduction

This chapter will set the scene for the remainder of the book by explaining some background theories and trends. It will expand our knowledge of management and the current market place by looking at particular situations which directly affect the professions. It will look at why some organisations succeed and others fail. It will develop a definition of "professional" which helps to illustrate how they behave and how they need to be managed.

2.2 Theories of management

Many management books are written for large organisations, typically producing products rather than services, operating as limited companies with formal structures of senior management, middle/supervisory management and staff. Senior managers spend their time on forward planning and strategies. Operational management is the responsibility of middle managers who seek to implement these plans on a day-to-day basis through co-ordination and control of resources and performance measures. Consistency of quality is achieved through standardisation of production. People are expected to adopt policies and procedures, and work within clearly defined roles and responsibilities.

Whilst many companies are leaner than they were in the 1980s and early 1990s, most continue to find the above approach useful. They now need to include more flexibility and innovation in what they do, but the basic approach continues to be valid.

Professionals do not comfortably fit into that style of approach. Most professional firms operate as partnerships rather than limited companies. Ownership, leadership and management are often combined. There are limitless variations in profit shares and operational structures. Professionals provide services to clients rather than products to customers. They tailor them to the needs of individual clients, making it difficult to compare one with the other. Measurement and standardisation is therefore of limited value. Professionals are by their very nature independent, and take responsibility for their own standards and training. They dislike any attempt to control what they do, considering that they are the best judges of the quality of their services. They will have little, if any, formal training in management and often see it as of secondary importance to them.

This highlights some of the issues which cause difficulty in trying to apply traditional management techniques to professionals and their organisations. This is not to say that such techniques have no value. Many of them can provide useful frameworks to help us to manage professional firms.

Most of the main writers on strategy emphasise the importance of matching the environment in which the organisation operates with its resources and the aspirations of its people (Porter, 1980, 1985; Wheelen and Hunger, 1989; Thompson, 1997; Johnson and Scholes, 1997). This holds true for both commercially orientated and not-for-profit organisations. More recently the emphasis has shifted to include the importance of allowing innovation and change within organisations – to allow them to adjust, respond and learn (Senge, 1990; Stacey, 1993; Kaplan and Norton, 1996).

Most theories encourage organisations to work through a process of carrying out analysis, identifying and selecting options, and then implementing them (Johnson and Scholes, 1997; Thompson, 1997) or "plan, decide, and act" (Stacey, 1993).

Marketing has shifted from a focus on product, price, place and promotion to being customer focused and responsive (Peters and Waterman, 1982; Peters and Austin, 1985). This has resulted in an emphasis on market research, customer feedback, and an acceptance that even product-based organisations need to identify which part of their customer service distinguishes them from their competitors.

Operational management theory concentrates on planning, controlling, co-ordination, monitoring and motivating (Child, 1984; Carson et al., 1995). This encourages organisations to make effective use of their resources – to introduce supply-chain improvements, such as just-in-time initiatives, and feed-back loops to identify any underutilisation or wastage.

The structure of an organisation has been identified as having a direct effect on its behaviour (Child, 1984). This has resulted in theories around "learning organisations" (Senge, 1990) as well as encouraging behavioural-change programmes. Mintzberg (1979), in particular, developed an in-depth analysis of operational structure. He considered five different styles – simple, machine bureaucracy, professional bureaucracy, the divisionalised form and the adhocracy. He provided a useful picture of a typical professional structure, such as seen in hospitals or universities, making distinctions between the behaviour of professionals and support staff. He also identified problems within that type of structure, such as interference by professionals in administration and difficulties of co-ordination between professionals. His work is perhaps one of the most comprehensive analyses of professional structures and continues to illustrate many of the problems currently faced in not-for-profit organisations in particular.

Such academic models and theories are therefore useful. Many merit detailed consideration and debate. This is not always possible for busy managers and professionals; but attempts should be made to keep up to date with new sugges-tions. Research, in particular, often provides examples of good practice which can be applied to particular situations.

2.3 The importance of understanding the market place

All organisations, whether in the public or private sector, are now directly affected by the external market place. Traditionally, the public sector could expect little change, with employees enjoying job security as a result. This has been eroded in recent years, with a growing emphasis being placed on budgets and achieving externally imposed targets. The private sector is feeling the pressure of the development of the global market. Companies outwith the UK are having a direct effect on our economy.

It is no longer possible to identify a strategy and stick to it, without consider-ing its continued relevance. The speed of change and the amount of information available have drastically increased the need for organisations to keep up to date with clients' demands and respond to them. The market place itself has expanded and continues to do so. This has resulted in customers and clients becoming more sophisticated and better informed. It is essential not only to understand and respond to this, but also to constantly adapt and alter the services and products we offer.

Even not-for-profit organisations need to understand their market place. For example, a charity dedicated to offering support to the elderly by providing accommodation to them has to be aware of the commercial growth in this area. This may have a direct effect on their potential client base as well as result in an increase in the standard of care that the market now expects.

This awareness of the market also reinforces the strategists' models of matching resources and people to the market place. Thompson (1997), argues that organisations can only operate in the area where all three overlap. If, therefore, the market place moves away from its current position, the other two must respond or the area of overlap will be reduced.

For example, the market has moved away from the acceptance of a table of fees for most professional services. This has resulted in downward pressure on fees, with firms having to improve their internal efficiency. One way to achieve this is to invest resources in computer support. However, some professionals are unwilling to adopt that approach, as they feel that it takes away from what constitutes a professional service. As a result, they are reluctant to invest in them and change the way they work. The market has moved away, but these firms and their resources are unwilling to follow it. This illustrates the need to constantly review and adapt as a result.

2.4 Why some organisations succeed and others fail

A great deal of research has been carried out into what makes organisations successful. Most highlight similar issues and provide key pointers for the remainder of this book. These include the importance of:

- using technical innovation to provide cost reductions (Hofer and Schendel, 1978);
- having flexible working practices and a focus for their activities (Davis et al., 1985; Milne and Thompson, 1986);
- aiming at product differentiation rather than price (Porter, 1985);
- operating in niche markets where they are regarded as market leaders (Davis et al., 1985; Richardson and Richardson, 1989; Burns and Harrison, 1996);
- favouring a planned approach, avoiding surprises, being aware of threats and opportunities and making good use of all of their resources (Robinson and Pearce, 1984; Richardson and Richardson, 1989);
- being lean, focused and innovative, having close customer contact and first-rate customer-support services, integrating technology effectively, seeking incremental investment rather than rapid expansion, and having a strong financial base (WINtech, 1990);
- being experienced in the sector, having established funding and a functionally balanced, proven and highly motivated management team and being forward thinking (Siegel et al., 1993);

- making good use of external advisors (Carson et al., 1995); and
- providing a high return on capital invested for their shareholders and working with positive cash flow (Burns and Harrison, 1996).

It is also worthwhile looking at what makes organisations fail. Again, research has been carried out in this area. Despite many perceptions to the contrary, most failures are related to internal problems rather than external pressures. Yes, there will be situations where the market place changes to such an extent that it is no longer possible to operate profitably; for example, where supply drastically exceeds demand or where tax advantages are removed. However, in most cases this could have been foreseen, providing opportunities for management to take decisions to reduce production and/or variable costs.

Failures are therefore mostly attributable to a failure of management. This can be the result of:

- a lack of skills per se, poor resource management, poor cash flow, taking on too much work, no forward planning, continuous firefighting, being internally focused and not responding to changes in customers' needs (Slatter, 1984; Boyle and Desai, 1991; Birley and Niktari, 1995).

It can also relate to an inability to manage change. The symptoms of this include:

- holding on to outdated products, being risk adverse, hoping by introducing price cuts to hold on to a share of an unprofitable market, and reluctant to let go of ownership and control (Miller and Friesen, 1984).

These are also the symptoms of a sector in decline and should trigger warning signs to some professional firms. Many of us have seen these types of responses to a decline in fee income; witness the reduction in fee levels for audit, conveyancing and survey work.

Other reasons for failure can be related to success. As organisations grow, the approach adopted when they were small will not necessarily work as they get larger. A typical example of this is small business start-ups where owners, often driven by a need to be independent, use their own money to develop a product that they want to make (Greiner, 1972; Churchill and Lewis, 1983). They carry out all of the functions of operational manager, marketing manager and financial manager themselves – or they may just muddle along! As they grow bigger, this will not be possible. They will need to learn to delegate and formalise some of their procedures rather than "carry them all in their head". They may need to borrow money from third parties, who will ask for written business plans. Not all companies make it through this transition and fail as a result.

Professional firms often mirror the situation described above with partners overcommitting to please their clients but reluctant to delegate to others. This can result in work not being completed on time, fees lying unrendered and clients complaining about poor quality of service. Cash flow and relationships then become a major problem!

2.5 What are professionals?

The main theme of the book is the difficulties that many of us experience when trying to work with and manage professionals. It is important for the sake of clarity to agree a definition of a professional from the outset. It also helps to build up a picture of why they can be difficult to influence using traditional management techniques.

Perhaps one of the easiest ways to develop this definition is to look at the elements which distinguish a profession from an occupation. These include that:

1. a profession is based on the application of specialist knowledge to a particular set of problems;
2. any entrant requires to have undertaken a period of training in both this knowledge and its practical application before seeking admission to his/her particular profession;
3. members are committed to continuous learning and upgrading of their expertise as well as training young professionals, often acting as mentors and role models;
4. it operates self-regulation of membership with entry being sought from and approved by other members, and disciplinary problems dealt with internally; and
5. it sees itself as providing a social service and contributing to the overall good of society.

A comprehensive analysis of the professions can be found in Torstendahl and Burrage (1990).

This definition indicates some of the issues which will be developed in later chapters. Internally, professionals enjoy considerable control over their own work, operating independently from their peers. They develop strong one-to-one relationships with individual clients, using considerable discretion and judgement when dealing with client issues. Externally, they tend to regard themselves as an elite group, as anyone who has sat in the company of barristers or surgeons will appreciate!

Working well, the professional model offers a collegiate group of individuals who:

- share expertise and support each other;
- adhere to a code of conduct which includes ethical behaviour;
- are committed to continuous development and self-improvement;
- put the interests of the public before their own; and
- honour the rules of their professional bodies over and above any personal or organisational demands.

Much of the current standing of the professions is based on their monopoly position and their influence in government. Both of these are being eroded. Self-regulation and restricted entry is now seen as self-serving, protecting the

2. Setting the Scene

incompetent professional from criticism or censure. Whilst their social contribution used to give them a certain standing and lobbying influence with government, recent governments of both parties have attempted to remove their monopolies. In addition, some professions are producing graduates in excess of what the market can sustain, with the number of lawyers, in particular, exceeding the amount of quality work available. This can cause dissension amongst those who value developing young people as well as being seen as a waste of resources.

Although their specialist knowledge provided the basis of their status in society in the past, clients have become more educated. More public access to professional knowledge has demystified their expertise and has provoked the ability to question the less than knowledgeable professional. Some professionals find it difficult to come to terms with clients challenging their advice.

In addition, negative elements have been highlighted with publicity given to the few "bad apples". Despite the fact that a very high percentage of professionals provide high standards of ethical behaviour, the media emphasises the bad examples. This results in a cynical attitude towards professionals with the social elements of their service being marginalised. It also results in external interference and recommendations about professional practice which, for the reasons outlined above, the professions take great exception to.

All of this has resulted in growing polarisation between what the professions see as their service to society and what society sees as overpaid monopolies. This is not a matter to be taken lightly. It poses serious and significant threats for the future, because once a profession no longer delivers the values of that society, there is a risk that it ceases to be seen as a "profession" (van Maanan and Birley, 1984).

2.6 What is happening in the professional market place?

When I meet with professional clients for the first time, many of them look tired and drawn. They often tell me that they simply do not know what to do for the better anymore. They know that the way they used to run their firms no longer seems to work. They know that they cannot continue to work this hard, continue to lose profits, continue to firefight in this way – but despite all their years of experience and dedication to their job, they can see no solutions to their current problems.

It is reassuring to be able to explain to them that their situation is not unique and is being experienced by many senior managers. Every sector and every area of society is experiencing change at an alarming pace, illustrated by the adjustments in the top 500 companies with the growth of "dot com" and e-commerce members causing waves of panic.

We cannot slow down this pace of change and revert to the "ways things used to be". We need to be able to respond to and manage that change. It is possible to analyse what we can control and influence – and what we cannot. This allows us to prioritise and focus our efforts and resources. The techniques to do this will be developed in later chapters, but we will start here by analysing the pressures currently impacting on the professional market place.

Professionals are right to be concerned. There are a number of significant trends which are directly affecting us at the moment. These include:

- client loyalty can no longer be taken for granted;
- the more educated clients are "doing more for themselves";
- traditional sources of fee income – such as audit, conveyancing and surveys – are not now profitable;
- younger professionals are no longer as attracted as in the past by the carrot of partnership;
- the market place is becoming increasingly competitive and overcrowded;
- technology is having a direct impact on the way that we work and the type of work that we do; and
- professional indemnity claims are on the increase.

The professional sector is under pressure in a way it has not experienced before. It requires a fundamental rethink of the way that we work and the services we deliver to our clients. We will need to learn new ways of managing our firms and the relationships that we build with our clients and each other.

On the positive side, however, it is now accepted that knowledge and its management will provide competitive advantage in the future. As technology increasingly replaces more routine tasks, people will have to move from being semi-skilled to skilled. Knowledge workers are more mobile than manufacturing workers. They tend to be more highly educated and better paid. The management of these people requires a different approach than that adopted in the past. As we have already discussed, the professions are, by definition, knowledge workers. As the market place demands more and more knowledge experts, this offers significant potential to develop successful professional organisations of the future.

As indicated above, it is important to be able to analyse the changes rather than simply feeling overwhelmed by them. One way to do this is to group them under a number of headings or influencers. This we will explore in more detail in Chapter 6. To set the scene, however, we will concentrate on two major areas which are having an important effect on all professions.

2.6.1 Technology

The impact of technology has had a significant impact on the way that we work. This is partly the result of increased communications with instant access now possible to most of the world. It also offers a wide range of possibilities of combining lifestyles with work and family.

It has meant that our market place has lost its traditional boundaries as people become more able to buy and sell goods regardless of their physical location. This has had a considerable effect on the professions where membership is restricted to geographical areas, such as Scotland or England, as clients now make demands to service their needs on a global basis.

The world is becoming "smaller", with differences in culture being eroded by brand images with teenagers in the USA and Far East choosing the same styles of clothes and music. This has increased the market place and power of the multinationals, who often appear to be above the confines of national governments. To counterbalance this, firms need to be aware of the strengths of their local connections and develop joint ventures and alliances with other localities to be able to compete competitively.

Specialist knowledge is now easily accessible to most people, with software development offering clients the opportunity to "do it themselves". Not only does this reduce potential fee income, it also serves to demystify professional expertise and encourages clients to be less intimidated by jargon and more confident to question professional advice.

The amount of information available is expanding at an alarming rate. Coupling this with the rapid pace of technological development means that it is increasingly difficult to maintain professional expertise. For example, the skills of the surgeon have changed dramatically with the introduction of keyhole surgery. Architects and engineers are now expert in CAD (computer-aided design) software developments. Even the most Luddite professional has had to learn how to access computer printouts! It is no longer possible just to read one or two journals to catch up with current developments. GPs are being offered a dedicated television channel to help them stay up to date. Many professionals now worry that they have significant gaps in their knowledge of what is current and good practice.

All sectors of society are becoming more and more dependent on information technology. Consider the extent and ramifications of the alarms caused by the worries over Year 2000 compliance. This is a trend that will continue with each generation more familiar with information technology than the previous. It has a powerful influence on the way that we live and do business.

For the professions, this has significant resource and intellectual implications. We will need to develop ways of investing in technology and continue to invest, as well as change the way that we work to respond to the potential that this offers – see Susskind's (1996/98) excellent work in this area. This will alter our skills mix and the shape of our organisations.

With the potential to access up-to-date databases of knowledge, we will need to change the way that we train people. We will no longer have to learn large tracts of information. Instead, we must be able to access and interpret that up-to-date information, which we apply to particular client problems. This requires a different way of training and a different set of skills. Some faculties are already responding to this, developing a "questioning rather than lecturing" approach to teaching students.

2.6.2 Consumerism

As already described in Chapter 1, some professions are experiencing an erosion of their preferred status in society. This is partly as a result of their reluctance to lose their monopoly position, which has put them on a collision course with government but also the result of increased consumerism. In addition, people are more likely to question and challenge their professionals than they were in the past.

This consumerism can be regarded as a positive influence. People should be able to question the advice they are given. Professionals should be encouraged to "keep on their toes" and provide high-quality services at all times. However, taken to extremes, this questioning can result in vexatious litigation. This increasing trend is forcing many professionals to adopt a back-covering approach to service delivery. It results in time away from working with the clients who do need help and a great deal of worry and concern for the professional affected. It also restricts the ability to make a "judgement call", encouraging the seeking of second and expert opinions, which adds to costs and further inflames the public outcry about charges!

It also results in an erosion of job satisfaction. I know of a number of high-calibre people who have retired from practice because of such an indemnity claim. Even when it was without foundation, the professional concerned often felt that he/she could have handled the matter better, usually by refusing to take on the client from the outset.

In addition, as clients have become more informed, they can do more for themselves. Non-professionals can now do routine business services, such as company formation or tax returns, resulting in an erosion of traditional areas of fee income, with a need to find replacement work.

As a result, the professional market place has become competitive with firms facing direct and indirect competition. Professionals are encroaching on each other's area of expertise, creating tensions between professional disciplines and a lack of concerted response. This is working against the identified trend described in Section 2.6.1 of the need to increase joint ventures and alliances to compete with increased globalisation. Whilst other sectors are adopting a partnership alliance style of approach, some professions are reducing the potential flexibility that this offers by putting up barriers to multidiscipline solutions.

2.7 What does the future hold?

The analysis of the above illustrates a number of important trends which we need to be able to manage and respond to. Whilst it is not possible to analyse these trends once and for all, it is possible to identify certain key themes:

- the pace of change will not reduce, with all sectors of our economy having to cope with continuous change;
- by nature, most people fear change and therefore exhibit certain defensive behaviour when faced with it;
- as people become more informed through increased access to information, the specialist knowledge of the professional will continually have to develop;
- professional skills of the future will no longer focus on knowledge itself but on its application to the needs of particular clients;

- professionals and their organisations must build on the strengths of professionalism not its weaknesses; and
- professionalism does have a critical role to play in the future success of our society.

As indicated in Section 2.4, triggers for change can come from both good and bad reasons. Some firms will want to change in order to stretch themselves and their people to develop higher values and/or more specialist services to clients. They may aspire to be market leaders, who set the example for others to follow. Others may have to change. They may be becoming less and less profitable every year, losing key people and seeing quality clients tempted away to other firms. In all professions, there is a continual need to improve our technical and specialist skills.

Whatever the reason, change is no longer an option. What we need to do is to be able to create an acceptance of change. Given people's natural reluctance to change and the effect of established behaviours, this is not easy to do. Yet, professionals and their organisations will have to change to survive.

2.8 The Model for Success

This book concentrates on success for professionals. We have already considered in detail what makes some organisations succeed and others fail. Successful professional firms are those which are focused and have a clear idea of where they want to be in the future. They excel in the services that they provide. As a result, they develop strong relationships with clients who value them and the advice that they provide. They have strong leadership, good management skills and encourage people to work well together. Partners concentrate on what they enjoy and delegate to and develop other people. Technology is integrated into the firm to allow it to provide high-quality services cost effectively.

These firms grow and continue to grow – not necessarily growing in size and/or turnover but instead growing in the sense of developing. This includes increasing people's understanding and skill base, increasing the balance between work and other aspects of life, and increasing individual health and well-being. It also means developing the organisation – increasing the quality of its clients and its services, thereby increasing people's job satisfaction and better serving the clients. This increases its profitability, creating the opportunity to better reward people for their efforts and invests in resources. With clients experiencing a high level of satisfaction, they will refer new business to it. This cycle of reward and satisfaction increases incrementally the organisation's potential future.

All organisations can therefore identify with the Model for Success. There will be those which want to stay the same size, but work less hard for the same or better return. Others will want to increase profitability by growing in size or specialism. In the public sector, growth in quality or reach of services may be the main driver, whilst in the commercial, it may be to serve the needs of internal clients in such a way that the influence of the professional within that organisation grows.

Each segment of the Model reflects an important aspect of organisations. Overall they allow us to achieve success.

2.8.1 Segment 1 Introduce effective management and leadership

This will be explored in Chapter 3. Effective management, which includes planning, decision making, controlling, organisation and motivation, must be introduced. To facilitate this, the organisation must have access to accurate, up-to-date information about the firm. However, professionals will only accept being managed by people that they trust and respect. We need to develop both of those elements in the way that we approach management and leadership. To do this, we need to go back to the core values of both our professionals and our organisation. Professionals will leave rather than compromise these values and will cause untold damage to working and client relations if they feel that these are under attack.

Many firms are reluctant to open a discussion on values because they are worried about airing sensitive issues. However, these values are fundamental to our beliefs and behaviour. In my experience, if these issues are not discussed, they will fester and resurface. Discussions will be blocked because people feel unhappy or threatened. Much time will be wasted with the firm unable to make decisions, let alone implement them.

2.8.2 Segment 2 Carry through an internal turnaround

The next stage is to carry through an internal turnaround (see Chapter 4). This requires a careful analysis of the resource base of the organisation – its people, clients, competitors, finances, service levels, systems and procedures. Some information will already be available, but other areas will require more investigation. Going though the process will increase people's understanding of the strengths and weaknesses of the organisation. Involving as many people as possible in the process will help to improve teamwork and communications.

The organisation needs to pose a series of questions. What is our current financial position? How is cash flow and profitability? Where is the profitable work coming from? Are people working at the right level? Are there areas of overload and underutilisation? How well are we using our time? Are there some clients we would be better off without? Are we all working to the same standards? How well are we using our IT systems? Have we used them to change the way that we work?

As a result of this, we may have to make some fundamental decisions about services we deliver. We may require to rationalise and reorganise. The way that people work may have to alter. The overall aim is to maximise the current resource base and increase the potential for future development.

2.8.3 Segment 3 Be client focused

Most professional firms place considerable emphasis on serving clients (see Chapter 5). They will feel therefore that they will already be "client focused". But they need to challenge that assumption by checking the self-diagnostic questions at the end of this book.

We need to look at the support that we offer clients. How easy is it to get hold of us? How approachable are we? We need to look at the way that we deliver our services. It may suit us to refer clients from one partner to another, but clients can be uncomfortable with this as they self-selected the professional that they have! We have to be careful not to damage that special relationship, both from the client-service perspective and from our firm development. Most of our new business comes from referrals from existing clients and connections. We need to be able to talk about money with clients!

In addition, we cannot assume that clients know the whole range of services that we can offer. Often we need to be more proactive in this area, by giving clients basic information about the firm. We need to understand what "selling" means in professional firms. We need to be client responsive but, at the same time, manage our own workloads and commitments.

We need to develop ways of identifying clients who value our services and those who do not. We may have to accept that there are some clients we are better off without!

To be competitive today, we have to do more than deliver a quality professional service. This is the minimum that clients now expect, and rightly so. We need to provide that additional "something" which makes us better than our competitors and adds value to the client relationship. As managers of professional firms, we need to create an environment which achieves this – where people work well together and share skills, expertise and client connections. We need the maximum contribution from all our people to achieve success for the firm.

2.8.4 Segment 4 Select and implement options

Chapter 6 will look at the process of identifying and implementing options for the firm. These must be based on an analysis of our values, which will continue to influence us whatever route the firm takes. Our current resources will provide the potential to implement these options, but we may need to identify additional resources in the future.

We need to develop ways of scanning the market place, not only to identify future trends, but also to identify opportunities. We need to learn to think creatively about the future and the potential it offers, even though the range of strategies open to us in some cases is limited by the current restrictions of our professional bodies. Options could include increasing market share, deciding on a niche approach to client services and/or taking our existing services into new markets. Other choices may involve joint ventures and alliances with other professionals, hiving off parts of the firm into specialist units and diversifying away from core services.

We need to sort out what is best for us – what will continue to deliver our values and maximise the potential that the firm has.

2.8.5 Segment 5 Shaping the firm

Chapter 7 looks at the shape of the firm – its structure and its people. Each organisation must develop the shape which suits it. Research into successful firms confirms that there is no "right" shape, only the structure which reflects the values of each particular firm and will deliver its picture of the future. Whatever operational structure is adopted, whether it be managing partner, management committee or practice manager, it must deliver effective decision making and most importantly implementation. It must also ensure the delivery of high-quality client services.

Each organisation has to devise and develop its own preferred style. It must also shape its people – allow them to grow and develop within the organisation. This may include reward structures and performance incentives. It may include career paths and clear models of what makes a good partner within the firm. Again, there is no template for this. It is up to the organisation to develop what suits and works for it.

2.9 Creating an acceptance of change

Working through the segments of the Model allows us to establish effective leadership and management, develop the resource and information base of the firm, ensure that our people deliver a valuable client service (for both parties) and identify our future strategies. We will have the right shape to maximise our current resource base and the potential to support us in the future. Overall, we will have and continue to have the ability to change as the demands of the market place and our clients.

We have established that the market place is changing at an alarming rate. Successful organisations are those that develop the ability to change and keep changing. It is no longer possible to set a strategy for future development and keep rigidly to it. Instead, businesses need to identify the way forward for them, set that in motion and then constantly review and adjust what they do. It is important to have a plan or a framework to provide a frame of reference, but that needs to be evaluated and adapted as required.

It is essential that we develop and maintain our ability to change. People generally do not like change as it often takes them out of their "comfort zone". It means that they have to learn new skills and ask for help. They will not be as productive for a while until they realign their skills and abilities. Organisations therefore are equally resistant to change. Change may mean short-term losses in the expectation of longer term gains.

Once firms have begun to work through the earlier segments of the Model, they will have become more comfortable with change. Some firms, however, are prone to too much change. Knee-jerk reactions to particular situations, such as cash flow or the loss of key clients can result in uncertainty about the future. People will become stressed and worried with the result that good people will leave and the remainder will become resistant to further change. Stress-related behaviour will develop which results in a "fight and flight" culture with people becoming difficult and challenging and blaming each other. Firms must be wary therefore of short-term responses to longer term problems and should take a measured and reasoned approach to decisions, based on accurate and up-to-date data.

Effective management requires the ability to manage change and continue to do so. This must be built on the establishment of trust and the processes of open communications and working with hard data. It also needs to be able to support people through that change, by allowing them to make mistakes and learn new ways of working.

CONCLUSIONS

Many professionals see little relevance in management and business strategies, partly as a result of their training and partly from the difficulties of applying them to the context of their particular challenges. However, such strategies can provide useful tools which can be adapted and put into practice.

Research illustrates the key elements of successful organisations. They are well managed and have strong resource bases. They are client focused and have a clear understanding of the market place and current trends. Professionals are by their very definition independent and articulate. The pressures imposed on them by the market place are significant and have a direct influence on current and future options. The Model for Success is designed to help them. It allows professionals to work through its individual elements of management, leadership, analysis, client focus and options, which combine to deliver the ability to change which is essential for their and their firms' survival.

 ## *KEY ACTION POINTS*

➢ Adapt traditional business techniques to suit our professionals and organisations

➢ Ensure that our values and resources meet the needs of the market place

➢ Constantly scan the market to check for current and future trends

➢ Watch for signs of failure in the organisation

➢ Develop an acceptance of change

➢ Work through each segment of the Model as this creates the ability to change and keep changing

3. Effective Management and Leadership

SHAPE FOR SUCCESS

EFFECTIVE MANAGEMENT LEADERSHIP

OPTIONS FOR DEVELOPMENT

INTERNAL TURNAROUND

CLIENT FOCUS

ABILITY TO CHANGE

ABILITY TO CHANGE

THE MODEL FOR SUCCESS

3.1 Introduction

This chapter considers the first segment of the Model for Success – the establishment of effective management and leadership. We have looked at the importance that effective management can play in the success or failure of our organisations. The skills of management are just as difficult to acquire as those of providing professional expertise. In most professional firms, management and leadership are often combined, which asks even more of those people tasked with running the business. In addition, professionals by reason of their background and training are not easy to manage.

This segment looks at the development of motivation and leadership, both of which are based on trust and respect. It develops ways of talking about our values, both professional and personal, and considers what happens when our values are not delivered. In this chapter, management will be broken down into its key elements of planning, implementing, organising and controlling. It also requires the creation of a culture which allows people to learn and adapt.

3.2 Why is effective management important?

We have already established that many business failures stem from a lack of effective management. This is supported by our experience in practice. If we think about the successful organisations we often envy, we know that they are well run, that they charge at competitive levels (if not higher) and are good at attracting new business and quality staff. This applies to the entire professional sector.

Effective managers must do more than ensure that the organisation runs smoothly. They need to provide leadership and a sense of cohesion as well as encourage innovation and change. Yes, they must be externally aware – aware of what is happening in the market place, of what clients need now and in the future. But they also need to be able to be equally skilled in internal operations and have the ability to run the business effectively.

Most professionals will have had a narrow technical education in their particular field. It is unlikely to have included any management training. Many will have had little experience beyond their own professional sphere. This results in a lack of understanding of what management entails. Many professionals do not see management as a "proper job". This reflects in their attitude and behaviour towards people who try to manage them. Some professionals would argue that the reason why I now concentrate on management is because I could not "cut it" in professional life! Yet, management is as difficult a skill as any professional discipline. It requires an understanding of fundamental concepts and principles, the ability to analyse them and their relevance, and to apply them to particular client situations. Not that much different from the work of full-time professionals!

This attitude towards management is also reflected in some of the approaches taken to management structures within firms. Some firms pay lip service to management by appointing the least able partner to the role of managing partner, on the basis that he or she can be most easily spared from client work. Others have compromised by appointing a partner for a term of, say, 2 years before getting back to doing client work. Others have set up committees who fit management around their "day job". None of these options accepts the importance of management and the role that it plays in the firm's success. Being an effective manager is just as important a job in a professional organisation as being a good professional.

However, some firms have accepted this importance. They have invested in management and extended the scope of their abilities (and attitude) by recruiting marketing, finance, IT and HR (human resource) professionals. This provides them not only with an enhanced skill base, but also a wider view of life outside professional firms. However, appointing these people alone is not enough. Partners must be prepared to listen to them and give them the status they need to do their job. Too often these "outsiders" leave after a few years frustrated by lack of progress and recognition of their value.

For example, one surveying firm appointed a senior manager from the oil industry as their managing partner. He had worked in an extremely competitive environment for over 20 years. He was a skilled and experienced manager well used to handling difficult people and situations. He left in despair after 18 months of dedicated effort, yet the firm describes his *appointment* as the worst mistake that it made!

There are many management structures that can be adopted. These range from committees, groups of partners, managing partners supported by non-partner teams and practice managers. There is no "correct" structure. Instead, each firm must work out which suits its style of operation. In addition, the question of the status of any "managers" has to be addressed. This has to include raising their credibility in the eyes of the core professionals. If non-partners are given responsibility for managing the firm's professionals, they must be given the authority and support to do so.

The firm will also have to consider the manager's future position in the firm. For example, a financial manager contributes significantly to the resource base of a successful law firm and wants to share in that success. If prevented by the rules of professional bodies from making that person a partner, how is that firm able to retain that level of commitment?

3.3 What is effective management?

The word "management" has many meanings and definitions. Fashions come and go as to what is effective management of an organisation. For example, Hickman and Silva (1987) in their review of management history describe that Era 1 (1910–1935) concentrated on the structure of organisations as the key focus for business development. It was replaced by "productivity" 1935–1955, "systems" 1955–1970, "strategy" 1970–1980, "culture" 1980–1985 and "innovation" 1985–late 1980s. In the 1990s, themes included teamworking, empowerment and knowledge management. These changes in emphasis can result in some degree of scepticism of management doctrines, especially where management consultants are concerned!

However, in my view, regardless of current fashions, the future success of any organisation depends on how well the aspirations of its people match its resources and the market place in which it operates. Effective management therefore requires first of all the identification of these aspirations and then the matching (and continual matching) of the resources of the business to the needs of the market place.

Managers need to be able to:

- identify where the organisation is at present and where it wants to go (plan);
- implement a plan of how to get there (implement);
- identify and source the resources it needs now and in the future (organise);
- ensure the resources are effectively used and developed (control);
- respond to any changes needed to sustain the match between current needs and future demands (adjust); and most importantly
- motivate people within the organisation to support all of the above!

We will look at these elements in more detail later in this chapter. To achieve them requires a wide range of knowledge and skills. These include an awareness of the market place and future trends, a detailed understanding of the firm, its resources and ways of working, of the people within the firm and their skills and abilities. Management also requires the ability to manage information, to analyse and conceptualise, to influence people and to manage and resolve conflict. Often, in large organisations, these skills are split between managers and leaders. However, within professional firms, managers and leaders are often one and the same! This asks a lot of these people and the difficulty of what they are trying to do must not be underestimated. This reinforces the importance of investing in professional management development.

3.4 Dealing with professionals

As outlined in Chapter 2, professionals pose a series of management issues. Because of their background and training, they have a limited understanding of management and what that entails. They can be quite dismissive of attempts to "manage" them. In addition, they have a strong need for independence and can be arrogant about their professional competence. They argue that every client situation is unique and needs a solution based on their particular skills and judgement. They can also be dismissive of people who do not directly contribute to service delivery. It is essential for the establishment of effective management that this type of attitude and behaviour is addressed.

One way to do this is to emphasise the importance of working *together* to provide a high-quality service delivery. It was pointed out in Chapter 2 that the market place and clients are becoming more demanding. It is now difficult to be an expert in every field. Professionals are having to work more co-operatively with other people (professionals and non-professionals) to provide a comprehensive client service. They need new technology to support them and access to information and training. All of this has to be funded and resourced. Professionals are being forced to accept that some co-operation and management is necessary to allow them to do their job! This is one way to encourage them to respond to being managed.

We have discussed that the aim of effective management for professional organisations is to ensure that clients receive a high-quality cost-effective service — now and in the future. Not only does this require that managers ensure a co-ordinated and cohesive resource base, it also requires people to work together and share their knowledge and expertise. It also implies that there must be some way of establishing an effective measurement of the quality of their output.

Some people will be directly involved in client delivery, others will not. We will explore in later chapters ways of measuring the quality of our services. There is a tendency for those involved in front-line work not to value the importance of other people. We need therefore to establish ways of measuring and rewarding the professional who helps others within the firm and the support staff who allow the firm to function effectively. For example, the development of a formal mentoring programme helps to raise the profile and status of this activity within the organisation. It should also identify direct benefits, such as increasing the overall skill levels and/or the retention and development of high-calibre individuals. Another way of achieving this is to set up multifunctional project teams which work on practical projects. This increases people's understanding of each other and the problems they face. All of this helps to support the messages of managers of the importance of working together to provide high-quality client services.

However, the test of effective management for a professional firm lies in its ability to *implement* any decision taken. This means that professionals have to be "bought" in to what the organisation is trying to achieve. Otherwise they will stall decision making and frustrate implementation. We will look at leadership and motivation shortly, but key skills are therefore those that facilitate decision making. These include the ability to:

- listen;
- create trust;
- motivate;
- influence without direct authority;
- create rapport;
- access and summarise information; as well as
- strong meeting skills.

These skills should not be alien to an effective professional experienced in working with clients! These skills must be reinforced by open communications and the involvement of everyone within the firm and, as discussed in this and Chapter 4, hard data.

Another skill is the ability to identify the people who are the key influencers within the organisation. They may not only be those who own the business. They may be people who, regardless of any formal position they hold, are influential in the way that decisions are made and more importantly implemented. For example, in any law firm, the cashier holds an important position of power and authority!

3.5 Motivation and leadership

Motivation encompasses the whole notion of leadership. The essence of leadership implies the ability to integrate people within an organisation – to ensure that people feel motivated to *work for* the organisation and *with* the other people within it.

As already indicated, it is often not possible within professional service organisations to split leadership and management. There may not be the resource base to allow people to concentrate solely on management issues. In addition, it is difficult and perhaps unwise to split it for another reason. Professionals will only be managed by people who they trust and regard as equals. This requires leadership skills from managers – of leading by persuasion and example.

3.5.1 Element 1 Discussing and agreeing values

As we have identified before, professionals place great emphasis on their values. These include both their own personal values and those of their professional bodies. Effective management requires first, the identification of these values and second, ensuring that the organisation delivers them.

This may seem self-explanatory and obvious common sense, but discussions about values rarely happen. Most organisations would see that as "too touchy feely" and fraught with difficulties. However, values are what drive and motivate professionals. Effective management requires the establishment of a way of talking about values and dealing with any conflicts or apparent conflicts.

3.5.1.1 What do we mean by values?

Values are those enduring principles that we hold dear and directly influence our behaviour. These can include higher values such as integrity and honesty, as well as more basic ones such as security and good health. One of the best ways to identify our own values is to consider why we left a previous organisation. What was it that finally made us say enough is enough? Was it that we were unhappy about the way other people were being treated (values of consideration, respect for others and teamworking)? Or that financial considerations appeared to be paramount (values of job satisfaction or duty to society)? Or that the firm seemed to be completely unaware of the importance of good management (values of security, trust and respect for others)?

Value conflicts can have a significant effect on us as individuals. They can be strong enough to make us leave an organisation. They can have a damaging effect on our health and well-being. Such conflicts can also have an effect on the organisation. It is important not only to develop a method of identifying individual and organisational values, but also to make sure that they are in balance.

3.5.1.2 The effect of value conflicts

Table 3.1 considers what happens when values are delivered. The groupings illustrate four areas – external values (i.e. those of the professional bodies), organisational values, personal professional values and private values. If those of the professional body are delivered, the firm will meet its compliance requirements, and enjoy a good reputation and image. It will also receive advice and support from that body, which may include notice of key trends and influences. If the organisation's values are delivered, it will have consensus, people will work well together, client service will be co-ordinated and effectively delivered, the organisation will be well resourced and have growth potential.

If the professional values of individuals are delivered, the organisation will enjoy commitment and energy from these people, who will share clients and

	Internal values	External values
Table 3.1 Values matrix – where values are delivered		
Organisational values	ORGANISATIONAL If delivered, have consensus, vision, resources, client satisfaction, growth	PROFESSIONAL If delivered, have compliance, support, reputation
Individual values	PERSONAL If delivered, have commitment, quality, job satisfaction, enjoyment, happy to share and develop others	PRIVATE If delivered, have health, balance, contentment

expertise. If private values are delivered, the firm will have healthy, balanced individuals who will be outward looking, innovative and responsive to change. It is important that all four boxes are in balance. No one should receive more emphasis than any other.

Table 3.2 considers what happens when values are not delivered. If the values of the professional body are not delivered, the organisation will suffer from complaints, rigorous inspections and a poor reputation. As a result, it will have difficulty in recruiting quality staff.

If the professional values of the organisation are not delivered, it will experience friction, poor communications and fragmented client support. If the professional values of individuals are not delivered, then there will be little sharing of expertise, a lack of trust generally with the good people (who can get positions elsewhere) likely to leave. With private values not delivered, people may have health- and stress-related problems.

	Internal values	External values
Table 3.2 Values matrix – where values are not delivered		
Organisational values	ORGANISATIONAL If not delivered, have friction, tensions, factions, lack of resources, poor communications with staff, fragmented client support	PROFESSIONAL If not delivered, have complaints, rigorous inspections, time taken up with responding, problems over recruitment of quality staff
Individual values	PERSONAL If not delivered, have stress, lack of trust, no openness or sharing of expertise, little creativity, bad behaviour and/or likely to leave	PRIVATE If not delivered, have health and stress problems

This analysis shows the importance of ensuring the delivery of values. This helps to illustrate our earlier discussions in Chapter 1 about the perceived dichotomy between being professional and being commercial, which stems from what appears to be a conflict over values. Many professionals think that business people are unethical and put their own needs above those of their customers. Professionals on the other hand work selflessly for ungrateful clients who give them nothing but problems! Couple all of this with a lack of understanding about what management entails and the normal defensive reaction to change and we begin to see why so many commercial decisions are blocked by professionals!

It is important therefore to debate and resolve any *apparent* conflict between the two. In my experience, if this "conflict" is brought out into the open, most of the issues can be resolved or may be based on a misunderstanding. This is often the first opportunity that people have to talk about this. The usual difficulty is getting them to stop talking about it! What starts out as a long list of alleged issues often dissolves into an enhanced understanding of the drivers behind the organisation as well as agreement on apparent areas of difficulty. To do this, firms can draw up two value boxes – those of commercial organisations and those of professional organisations and then compare the two. There will be many similarities. Both will value high-quality client delivery, both will value the skills and expertise of their people, both will value the resources to support that.

For example, managers are looking for their professionals to use their judgement to provide a quality client service. Professionals want managers to support them by providing trained staff and sufficient resources to allow them to perform their role effectively. It is therefore in both the organisation's and the client's best interests to ensure that the firm is run commercially. No manager of a professional service organisation would want his or her professionals to compromise his or her professionalism as this would make no commercial sense in an organisation dedicated to high-quality service.

3.5.1.3 How to identify our values

First of all, the whole issue of values needs to be explored. This may appear to be too nebulous an area to start with but it is essential. Even with existing relationships within successful organisations, their values should not be assumed. It should be easy to articulate them and get them down on paper. As indicated before, this will provide a useful mechanism for recruiting the "right" people. In addition, it is important to address any false assumptions.

For example, one accountancy firm I worked with was experiencing tensions between the partners. I was called in to help them make progress with implementing their plans to expand the client base. I inherited a large file, full of consultants' reports and action plans. All seemed useful and relevant, yet no progress was being made. On investigation, it was apparent that the partners had made some assumptions about each other. One of the younger partners appeared to want to grow the firm quite aggressively. One of the more senior partners had actively chosen in the past to leave a larger firm because he was unhappy with its values.

He assumed that these were the values of all larger firms, and therefore, of his young partner. He was blocking any attempts to grow the firm, using all of the indirect means at his disposal! Once we openly discussed and agreed the values of the firm together, both partners realised that the firm could develop within that framework. Progress is now being made. Many key actions have been completed, new work is coming in and all the partners are working well together.

What can we call this framework of values? The phrase "mission statement" has developed a fairly bad press in recent years, with people feeling that the words often bear little relevance to the reality of working in that organisation. However, the creation of such a frame of reference is important as it forces an organisation to reflect on what is core to its beliefs and values. Rather than talk about "mission statements", I prefer discussions around "commonality of purpose". This encourages people to talk about why they work together, what is important to them now and in the future. This gets away from problems over whether we have a "mission" *and* a "vision" statement! These frames of reference, by their very creation, will be personal to individual organisations. However, there are often generic elements which include:

- *we are committed to supplying high-quality (professional) support to clients;*
- *we work with clients who value what we do for them;*
- *we care about our patients and our people;*
- *we adopt a creative approach to client services;*
- *we will be known for our creativity and design;*
- *we value everyone's contribution to service delivery;*
- *we invest in our people to allow them to maximise their potential;*
- *we believe in teamworking and reward people accordingly;*
- *we are committed to our role in the local community;*
- *we will ensure the future viability of the organisation.*

Key words are often quality, professional, efficient, innovative, profitable, resourceful, balanced, caring, responsive, partnership, client focused and community. If there are apparent disagreements about values, it is important to agree the *fundamental* values which will provide the frame of reference for future discussions and decisions. These "fundamentals" can consist of a list of core values, which everyone adheres to.

In an existing professional relationship, any disagreement over values must be addressed and resolved. Otherwise, these issues will surface in other discussions and prevent decision taking and implementation. In a fledging professional relationship, it is important to establish agreement on fundamental values at the outset.

The values of the organisation and the individuals working within it must be the same. There is a tendency to assume that all professional partnerships will have the same values (i.e. quality, integrity, financial robustness), but in practice this is not the case. For example, some professional organisations will rank teamworking much higher than others, and will, as a result, prefer to accept lower income levels to preserve the team. Others will place delivering high-level specialist services over attracting more lower level work.

First of all, the firm should generate a list of values. This can be done in a number of ways; for example, by looking through any promotional material of the firm and highlighting the value words used. It can also be done by listening to the way that people talk about the firm and how they describe it. This exercise can include staff, clients and other organisations. They will use certain keywords to describe what is special about the firm and/or what makes it different from other similar firms.

This list should be debated and agreed on. If there is a wide range of suggestions, this could illustrate a problem which will need to be debated and resolved. This debate will involve asking people to articulate the reasons why they chose one over another, which helps to increase everyone's understanding of what is important to individuals.

Another way of generating a discussion about values especially at partner level is to ask people to write down what a "good partner" would look like. This will produce a list of attributes, such as good teamworker, good at developing client relations which can be further broken down into a list of values (this picture of a "good partner" is developed in more detail in Chapter 7).

3.5.1.4 Talk about money!

We have already argued that one aspect of professionalism is an unwillingness to ascribe financial reward to the delivering of services to clients. This leads to a general reluctance to talk about money even internally. However, we need to become business focused in the way that we manage our firms. It is important that the financial side of the firm is discussed and that people have an overall understanding of it – of cash flow, of profitable clients and areas of work, of costs and overheads.

For example, lying out time means lying out money. The importance of this can be reinforced many times to professionals without any apparent effect on their attitude to fee recovery! In addition, professionals are fundamentally uncomfortable about talking money. There are a variety of reasons for this which include that money is often not a motivator for professionals. In addition, they feel that putting a price on their judgement alters the client–professional relationship. Instead of the client coming to us for help, which we are kind enough to give, the client pays us for services received. This shifts the power of the relationship to that of equals!

Whatever the validity of these reasons, they influence the way that professionals deal with and discuss money. The client's perception is often the opposite! Consider the publicity that GPs suffer, allegedly taking patients off their list as a result of expensive drug costs; or of "fat-cat solicitors milking legal-aid fees"!

Not everyone in the organisation needs to become an accountant, but senior people, in particular, have to become more comfortable with finance and figures. In addition, the organisation needs to be able to access accurate and up-to-date financial information. The importance of this cannot be overestimated as it allows discussions at partners' meetings to be based on objective facts, rather than subjective opinions. This makes a considerable difference to their temperature and length!

If finances can be discussed routinely on the basis of accurate and relevant information, everyone will become more comfortable with the discussion, with the firm able to respond to issues on a rational basis. It will improve everyone's understanding of the firm's position as well as helping people to become more comfortable about talking about money in general. As a result, they will become better informed and more skilled in talking to clients about fees and fee levels (see the importance of that in Chapter 5).

3.5.2 Element 2 Developing trust

The essence of any partnership is trust. This is also becoming increasingly important for organisations involved in joint ventures and alliances, who have to develop partnerships with other businesses and operations.

Many management books in recent years have debated the differences between a leader and a manager, arguing that their roles are distinct yet complementary. Whilst this may be the case for large organisations where leaders lead and managers manage, within the professions this can cause real difficulties. As outlined above, professionals will only work with people that they trust. In addition, they resent any attempt to directly control their work – "managing people is like herding cats" (see Bennis 1998 on leadership). This reinforces the need for managers to inspire trust rather than impose control and takes us back to earlier comments about the need to deliver values and generate that trust.

The leadership skills of inspiring trust are difficult to define. We all know that there are some people we inherently trust and others who, from the outset, we are uncomfortable with. A lot of this stems from the value discussion outlined above. *We trust people who have the same values as we have.*

How do we know whom we can trust? How do we access that information? We can formally debate values as discussed above. But we often do it in an additional way. We look at people's past performance and track record. We have already identified that professionals have strong "closed shop" networks. This means that we can find out the history of people – often knowing who they worked with in the past, which organisations they trained in and the type of client services they have been involved in. We are able to quickly tap into first-hand knowledge of that individual and his/her "professionalism" and are therefore much more likely to trust people we can trace in that way.

This partly explains the difficulty that non-professionals, or professionals from other disciplines, have when trying to manage professional firms. Professionals like to use jargon, often as a shorthand way of communicating but also as a way of assessing people's understanding of them. They argue that outsiders do not understand them and their problems. Again, they are more willing to trust people who "speak their language", illustrating that it is often easier to train professionals in management than the other way round! Without working with them for many years, it is not easy for external managers to convince professionals of their worth.

As with any relationship, one of the best ways of developing trust is by being willing to listen to people. Managers and leaders should place a lot of emphasis on this. However, listening is not enough. Having listened, effective management requires a response – based on reasoned analysis and consistent judgement. Good managers must seek to be respected, not liked!

Open communications are another important element in the establishment of trust. This is one of the most difficult management issues for most organisations. Even those who put enormous efforts and resources into communication processes are still criticised by staff for a failure to communicate. Some large organisations have developed intranets, newsletters, staff forums, "away days", off-site conferences and yet, staff surveys will still score low on effective communications! Whatever sector is involved, people at all levels in the organisation *always* place most emphasis on direct, face-to-face communications from senior management who take the time to talk to them.

The importance of managing through trust cannot be overestimated. Not only does it link directly with the importance of delivering shared values for the organisation and the individuals within it, but also it makes the process of management much easier. It avoids the need to impose controls which can take up so much of management time. It also allows the development of learning and innovation which is so important in today's highly competitive market place.

Having looked at the first and crucial element of effective management, Section 3.6 now considers the next element – planning.

3.6 Planning

Inadequate management results in an inability to react to changes in the market place, to provide the resources needed to operate effectively and to plan ahead. Research indicates that businesses which engage in a formal planning process perform better in the long term. Planning is therefore an important exercise and provides a number of direct benefits to the organisation and its management.

Especially within partnerships, planning can give a sense of cohesion and a common purpose with written plans providing a frame of reference against which to make short- and long-term decisions. This will, in turn, facilitate both implementation and the ability to change. It also encourages the consideration of what resources are needed and how these should be allocated and co-ordinated. This in turn increases productivity and awareness of the cost and benefits of these resources. In addition, formal plans can be useful to obtain external funding and support.

Planning implies a structure and a logical approach to where the firm is and where it wants to go. Not all planning needs to be formal, but I would recommend that for professional firms, where there are a number of owners, it is important to formalise what is agreed in writing and quickly. I can think of one situation where the firm's partners and I spent the morning agreeing their long-term strategy and short-term objectives. After I and one of the other partners left, the others stayed on and talked themselves out of it!

Table 3.3 Business plan	
A suggested index for a business plan should include:	
Heading 1 Introduction	
Heading 2 Where are we now?	
An analysis of the current firm including:	see
• Our values	Chapter 3
• Our strengths, weaknesses	Chapter 4
• What services we provide	Chapter 4
• Our people and their expertise	Chapter 4
• Our structure and systems	Chapter 4
• Our current resource level	Chapter 4
• The clients we serve	Chapters 4/5
• Our direct and indirect competitors	Chapter 4
• Market-place opportunities	Chapter 6
• Market-place threats	Chapter 6
Heading 3 How well have we performed in the past?	Chapter 4
Heading 4 The current and future market place	Chapter 6
Heading 5 Where do we want to be in the future including	
• Our commonality of purpose	Chapter 3
• What we should look like?	Chapter 6
• What people will be saying about us?	Chapter 6
• How will we know that we are successful?	Chapter 6
• Our long-term objectives	Chapter 6
Heading 6 How are we going to get there?	
• Our short- and medium-term objectives	Chapter 6
• Our people skills and other resources	Chapter 7
• An outline of financial targets	Chapter 6
• Our key performance indicators	Chapter 6
• What changes we need to make	Chapter 6/7
• Resource implications (both financial and other)	Chapters 6/7
• Our Action plan	Chapters 4/6
Heading 7 Financial Projections	

There is no absolute template for a written business plan, but the general headings should include (see Table 3.3):

1. an introduction to the firm, what makes it different from others/competitors, including our commonality of purpose/frame of reference;
2. an outline of the current business including what business are we actually in, what are our values, our products/services, our strengths and weaknesses, our people, structure, systems and resources;
3. a review of our past performance;

4. a review of current and future market trends, including our clients and competitors;
5. a vision including our long-term strategic objectives;
6. a practical action plan of how we are to get there which includes resource implications (both financial and other) and critical success factors/key performance indicators;
7. financial projections.

This appears at first glance to involve a lot of work. However, the plan can be built up over time and once the first one has been completed, it is a much quicker task to keep it up to date and agree future plans. The segments of the Model for Success facilitate the development of the plan. For example, this chapter provides the "commonality of purpose" and skills to agree and implement the plan. Subsequent chapters help with headings 2 to 6.

However, the planning *process* itself is as important as the written plan. The process allows the firm to debate, identify options, analyse and prioritise. This helps to develop management skills and the overall understanding of the organisation.

As with any service-related business, the people aspect of planning is important. Not only must the firm have the current skills and knowledge required, it must also be able to identify and develop its future "people needs". This may require additional skills, or the development of a different type of skill, such as computer literacy and/or para-professionals.

For any plan agreed by the firm, there must be two inherent elements. First of all, the plan must be agreed fairly quickly and reviewed regularly. There will never be a perfect plan as both the internal and external environments change on an ongoing basis. The plan must therefore be flexible and able to react effectively to changing circumstances and opportunities. The second, and equally important, element is that people feel that they have ownership of the plan. Without that, they may pay lip service to it but they will not put it into practice.

3.6.1 The process

The process of planning starts with agreement of what makes the firm "special" or different from other firms and/or its competitors. This allows discussion about values and commonality of purpose. Any plan must include an analysis of where the firm is now and where it wants to be.

This creates the frame of reference against which decisions can be taken. It is important to formalise this in writing to confirm what was agreed. Not only does this ensure that the firm keeps on track, but also it ensures that later discussions keep to the subject. This helps to reduce the time taken in partners' meetings by achieving some focus for agenda items and decisions!

This is an important point as partnership structure provides endless opportunities for debate and consensus seeking. Couple this with professionals' tendency to debate points as a matter of principle and it is not hard to see why partnership meetings often get nowhere! In addition, there is now a need to move faster than in the past. All organisations need to be able to change and change quickly. The average speed of partnership decision making is now too slow for current market demands! It is important therefore to be very focused about what decisions are taken and how they will be implemented.

We can all think of many examples of poor and ineffective decision making by professionals. One firm I know spent a great deal of time agreeing whether to buy an existing firm in a nearby town. Many special meetings were called, accounts were looked at, lease terms examined. Eventually the decision was taken to buy, against what was by now out-of-date financial information. Then and *only then*, it was discovered that no partner was prepared to take operational responsibility for the new office, least of all, actually go and work there!

Many management consultants refuse to work with professional firms because of the time that it takes for them to make a decision! Yes, we need consensus but not everyone needs to be involved in every decision. The development of a plan therefore helps the process of decision making and delegation. Once the overall direction has been identified, it is much easier to delegate and give people the authority to take action.

Again, it is important to be aware of both the decision makers *and* key influencers within the organisation. Remember that there will be people who may not be part of the formal decision-making process who will have an influence on both the decision taken and subsequent implementation. They also will need to be effectively managed – persuaded to support the decision rather than work against it.

3.6.2 *The importance of accurate, up-to-date information*

The process of planning requires the sourcing of hard data. This will be explored in detail in Chapter 4. The generation of accurate and up-to-date information about the firm, its clients, profitability and resource base facilitates decision taking by allowing people to talk from an objective rather than subjective point of view. It is important that people within the firm need to understand at least the basic elements of accounting. All organisations should carry out some basic training in this area for all of their professionals. Such concepts as break-even analysis, and fixed and variable costs are useful tools to illustrate fundamental financial concepts and allow the firm to plan and make decisions based on hard facts about current workloads and future-development options.

Critical success factors or key performance indicators should be built in, such as the spread of work or dependence on key clients. These should extend beyond finance alone and include some qualitative measures of success, such as new business won and/or profile-enhancing achievements. They should be as measurable as possible and provide comparisons over time, against budgets, other departments and/or against external standards. As indicated earlier, it is important that there is some measurement of people who help and develop others.

They should also relate to the future objectives of the organisation, otherwise it is too easy to make short-term decisions at the expense of longer term options. If possible, compare performance with that of other organisations, either in the same or other sectors. Worthwhile information can often be obtained from professional bodies who have data on trends or performance levels in general. In all cases, any indicators selected must be readily understandable by those affected by them.

They can also help to "control" the firm with routine reporting highlighting areas of over- and underspend, allowing a constant eye to be kept on the firm's performance in general. If at all possible, these reports should be visual – such as coloured pie charts – which makes them much easier to look at than a list of figures and helps people to understand them quickly. Such reporting should happen monthly rather than quarterly, as this enables the firm to respond in good time to any changes required. The discipline of producing information monthly means that the firm has to limit the amount issued to what is relevant and important.

Involving as many people as possible in the process of planning is essential. The plan should not and cannot be prepared by an outsider. The process of planning requires an understanding of the underlying elements, analysis of what is relevant and what is not, the generation of options and agreement on priorities. Working through this increases everyones understanding of the firm, its drivers and what is important to it. It also increases the "buy-in" to the plan, by allowing debate and agreement. It therefore improves its chances of being implemented!

3.7 Implementation

Implementation is the ultimate test of effective management. As already commented upon, too often partners may intellectually commit to a decision, but when it impacts on them as fee earners, they will not follow it through. This does considerable damage to the credibility of management. Younger professionals and staff see partners spending hours in meetings to agree certain key development activities, read memos and e-mails which advise them of changes within the practice and then see those same partners ignoring these changes and carrying on in the way that they have always worked regardless. Even worse, some partners may openly discuss their lack of regard for the agreed plan or initiative thus further undermining management (both the personnel and the concept).

Agreeing a frame of reference and a plan helps to "enforce" implementation. Few sanctions exist within professional organisations where many of the professionals are also the owners of the business. Managers can refer back to the framework of what was agreed to remind the professionals that they have committed to that course of action for the *benefit* of the firm and its clients. It is vitally important not to let individuals slide out of implementation as this will encourage others to do likewise, which reflects the importance of the consistent leadership.

We have considered that the key to effective management of professionals lies in the creation of trust and agreed common values. These values have to be the point of reference in all decision making and in subsequent implementation so that failure to follow through on a decision is seen as a breach of trust and a non-honouring of values. This may seem an extreme approach to encourage people to keep databases up to date but if we remind professionals that we need to do this to ensure good quality client service then they are more likely to do it than if they are told to!

The whole process of decision making and implementation should also be supported by the operational structure adopted by the organisation. This relates to Section 3.8 — that of organising.

3.8 Organising

Effective management requires the ability to organise the resources of the firm, which implies identification of what resources are needed and where they are to be found. This may include additional resources that need to be "bought in" as well as increasing the internal resource base by better planning and organisation. There are two elements of resources — first, physical resources, such as premises and equipment, and second, softer resources, such as people's skills, knowledge and, equally important, their attitudes. This reflects the comments above concerning their "buy-in" to the agreed plan and its implementation.

A good deal of management time will be taken up with these "people" issues. Their organisation will require activity around relationships and communications. It also introduces the importance of delegation, which will be considered in more detail in Chapter 4 when we consider the internal workings of the firm. For a firm to be effectively organised, the right people should be doing the right work at the right time in the right way. In other words, the firm needs to ensure that the resources of the firm are being used to their maximum potential.

Any organisation of resources also has to allow the resources to develop. In the case of people, that implies that they will need to learn and adjust — to make mistakes and be supported in that learning. This is important because too often organisations adopt a "blame culture", resulting in little innovation and development. It also results in people being unwilling to take responsibility and hiding mistakes. I know of a number of occasions where, some months after individuals have left, mistakes have come to light which lead to indemnity claims. Many could have been resolved if they had been admitted to when they occurred. Again, this ties back to the importance of trust. When I was an apprentice, I worked with a partner, who demanded high standards of me. However, if I made a mistake, he accepted responsibility for it with the client. I respected him for that and trusted and worked hard for him. Firms must work hard at reducing any attempts to blame people for mistakes and seek to develop an open culture which allows learning and development.

3.9 Control

Effective management requires the control of resources (both physical and people) and the services they provide. This is not easy for a number of reasons. As highlighted in Section 1.9, professionals consider themselves to be independent and judges of their competence and client delivery. They argue that they must use their professional judgement in every case and in every client situation that they deal with. Managers cannot nor ever will be able to "control" professionals by policing them. Given that the handling of a client file or matter requires judgement, there are many grey areas. This reinforces the importance of direct experience of the job when it comes to managing professionals. Hospital doctors, for example, are much more able than their managers to judge what is required for essential patient care. They have developed skills in "shroud waving", insisting that any compromise will affect people's lives!

This does not mean that managers should abdicate control. Effective control requires that good and reliable information is available. In addition, it should involve the introduction of as much standardisation as is useful to the firm. The extent that standardisation is possible will depend on the nature of the services provided. Control of fairly routine work will be improved by the introduction of checklists and procedures. It should also improve the efficiency with which the work is carried through, making it easier for less qualified people to undertake the work. The ultimate aim of developing any standardisation is to achieve consistency of service *and* improve efficiency. It is quite common to see processes introduced which may help consistency but reduce efficiency and vice versa!

Managers should encourage the establishment of key policies and procedures and monitor their effectiveness. It is essential to unbundle those elements of the service which are core and/or consistent in every client project and those which are not. Most firms are able to define the core of their client services and develop "standards" of service delivery.

Quality standards and processes were in vogue throughout the late 1980s and 1990s with the ultimate goal of improving consistency through the formalisation of work practices. Whilst this formalisation may have value for professionals, it must be used with care.

Professionals must use their own judgement as the needs of clients are different and varied. This process cannot become prescriptive and is therefore difficult to standardise. Whilst computerisation has helped a number of professions, such as architecture and surveying by reducing the time taken on drawings and producing costings, it has not taken away from the professional skills involved.

There are areas where formalisation is valuable; for example, where the organisation is seeking to delegate work to non-professionals. Routine work can be broken down into checklists and core steps. However, within the scope of the performance of professionals it is not easy to prescribe each element of client service. As a result, there will always be situations where it is better to motivate people to work effectively at the same time as allowing them to tailor the service provided to individual clients.

The content of policies and procedures should be agreed by the firm and can be as detailed as the firm is comfortable with. These can include basic procedural guidelines, client checklists and, more increasingly, customised software packages. Care must be taken to ensure that this formalisation does not take away from ensuring that the overall service continues to meet the professional needs of clients. For example, style documents should not be used without being checked. Professional judgement will always be needed at some stage of the file and should not be abdicated.

One of the most important policies to develop is a "feeing policy". Effective management will aim to encourage professionals to understand the importance of good cash-flow management. Commitment to this can be bought by revisiting people's values and the importance of good client service through investment in technology, office premises and trained staff or whatever else will assure the buy-in of key people. A good manager will always know the Achilles heel of each of the key influencers within the organisation!

The establishment of a feeing policy illustrates one of the particular problems facing managers of professional organisations. Managers of typical product-based organisations will be able to base their prices on well-defined principles of operational costs and/or competitor positioning. Our firms however, do not have tangible products to produce and compare. We must develop ways of identifying the cost of different services, what our competitors are charging and what clients are prepared to pay. This allows some basis for setting fee levels. In addition, the firm needs to agree policies about when a client should receive a fee. Tradition has established that this is paid for in arrears which means that we have to lie out our time and pay attention to work-in-progress values. These points will be developed in Chapter 4.

A "communication policy" should also be established. This can be as formal or as informal as the organisation decides, but there are a few key essentials. It should include everyone – all levels, all departments, professionals and non-professionals. It should aim to deliver consistent and accurate information, and provide as much detail about the organisation, its future plans and *finances* as the partners/senior managers will tolerate. People are able to make the connection between money and future success. Where people are informed in this way, they feel that the organisation trusts them and is looking for their contribution to help in its success.

Control of existing resources is important. Equally important is the continued development of these resources, which often involves short-term inefficiencies to achieve longer term gains, as anyone who has been involved in the introduction of a new computer system will appreciate! This may mean on occasions allowing people to "waste" resources – waste time learning new skills or taking time away from client services to explore new opportunities and/or develop outside connections.

3.10 Adjust and respond

It is important to remember that effective management is a continuing process. It requires constant adjustment to changes within the firm and externally within the market place. This reflects the importance of agreeing a frame of reference – an umbrella under which the firm can adjust and respond. Regular review processes need to be established which should include all the resources of the organisation – its people, systems and procedures. These should be used to highlight areas of underperformance, of poor delivery or of changes in demand. Managers need to stay on top of the overall quality of the firm's output and constantly develop its resources to support its future.

CONCLUSIONS

Establishing effective management and leadership is the first step for any organisation in developing its ability to change. There is no "right structure" to help to achieve this. Some firms will allocate responsibility for managing to an individual or group of individuals. Some will separate management and leadership. Others will work successfully through the recruitment of external experts.

Whatever shape is adopted must suit the values and attitude of the firm. The values of a professional firm drive it forward. These need therefore to be identified and supported. Management implies the ability to plan, implement, organise and control. However, to be fully effective, managers must also be leaders. They must be able to inspire trust and motivate people.

KEY ACTION POINTS

➢ Remember that leadership and management are one and the same thing

➢ Make sure that the organisation understands the importance of being effectively managed

➢ Whatever structure is adopted must deliver implementation of decisions

➢ Accept that professionals are not easy to manage

➢ Manage professionals through their values rather than by imposing controls

➢ Watch out for any apparent conflict between "commercial and professional" values

➢ Talk about money

➢ Develop trust and open communications

➢ When developing the business plan, involve as many people as possible

➢ Agree a "frame of reference" for the organisation

➢ Make sure the firm has accurate and up-to-date management information

➢ Establish key performance measures which assess current performance and future potential

➢ Develop standards, policies and procedures where they improve efficiency and consistency

➢ Accept that effective management is a continuous process.

4. Turnaround to Best Practice

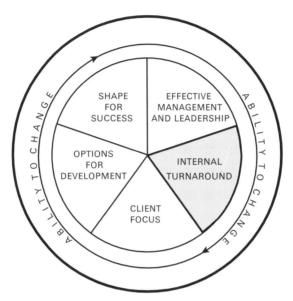

THE MODEL FOR SUCCESS

4.1 Introduction

As we have established, many organisations fail to develop as a result of a lack of effective management. They have limited understanding of management and what that entails. This includes a lack of understanding of pricing, overheads, working capital, cash flow and/or of the quality of services or products. Some fail because they overtrade – because they take on too much work and/or work which is unprofitable for them. They confuse being busy with being successful. Others fail because their owners are inflexible and autocratic, refusing to seek outside advice.

Good management requires the effective use of all of our resources. This chapter encourages us to have a better understanding of our resource base – our people, finances, service levels, systems and clients. It also encourages firms to look at their quality and identify where and how they differ from their competitors. As with Chapter 3, the process of this analysis is as important as the outcomes. It allows people to increase their understanding of the firm, and its strengths and weaknesses. Working through this process helps the firm to turn around to meet future demands upon it.

4.2 What do we mean by "turnaround"?

Within this chapter, the phrase "turnaround" describes the next segment of the Model. Accountants often use this phrase when called in to work with a client organisation experiencing trading difficulties. Their emphasis, by necessity, is on providing a fast effective short-term solution to these problems, with the result that they tend to focus on cost-cutting and overhead reductions. However, this chapter encourages a wider and longer term turnaround strategy which consolidates the organisation as well as increases the resource and knowledge base for future development activity.

To move forward, any organisation needs an established resource base. This has to include not only the traditional hard resources of balance-sheet assets, such as capital and equipment, but also the softer resources of good communications and working relationships. The organisation needs to be aware of its strengths and weaknesses, of its external market opportunities and pressures. This requires careful analysis of all aspects – its systems and people, working capital, client base and future potential.

4.3 Open and informed discussions

To discuss these strengths and weaknesses will inevitably mean that sensitive issues within the organisation will need to be explored. As outlined in Chapter 3, one of the key elements of effective management is the establishment of trust and open communications. Partnerships by their very nature rely on trust, with the result that difficult discussions are often avoided. Unless of major significance, there is a perception that opening that particular "can of worms" may not be worth the tension and friction that it will cause. Most partners tell me that they often do not raise issues for this very reason, and cite a number of examples of quite fundamental problems within the firm they are already aware of, but which they are reluctant to talk about. These can include feeling unfairly treated about current fee targets and knowledge of client service problems.

However, in my experience, failure to talk about such matters can be just as damaging. These issues will fester and cause underlying problems. To turn the firm around, we need to look at good *and* bad working practices and relations. Areas of future work and workloads need to be identified and supported. This may appear to threaten current expertise and client delivery, but it is essential that these areas are explored otherwise the organisation will not be able to develop. It will often be stuck with out-of-date skills and entrenched attitudes.

Most professional partnerships baulk at the idea of addressing these sensitive issues, but we need to develop a way to do this. The best way is to work from factual information, rather than people's perceptions. We need to gather as much data as possible to be able to discuss these issues from a *basis of fact*. Yes, some of us will instinctively know what needs to be done, but obtaining hard data allows these areas to be discussed objectively rather than subjectively. In addition, such analysis creates a range of options to be weighed and decided on. This provides the benefit of depersonalising the debate, which is extremely important in dealing with partnerships where any erosion of trust can be damaging.

4.4 The starting point

One of the best ways to start is for the organisation to complete the traditional SWOT analysis (this common-sense checklist has been used for many years; e.g. see Tilles, 1968), which considers the internal strengths and weaknesses of the organisation and its external opportunities and threats. This is a fairly easy exercise and should not become time consuming. It should be completed by everyone who has a financial and/or professional interest in the firm (i.e. the partners and senior managers, younger professionals, support staff, external contacts, clients, patients or customers). It is not always possible to involve everyone but it is important to provide as wide and as comprehensive a review as possible as everyone's perceptions are valid. Also, this exercise starts to open up communications and build commitment from everyone.

An example of a typical professional firm is shown in Table 4.1.

Table 4.1 SWOT analysis	
STRENGTHS	WEAKNESSES
Well established	Traditional fee areas declining
Wide range of services	Not specialised
Premises well sited and good of appearance	
Loyal and stable staff	Traditional skills now out of date
Wide client base	Lack of client awareness of all services
Good range of partners – age and expertise	Now large firm – needs restructure
Good reputation	Current work levels too high
Operates efficiently	Communications poor
Good working relations	Decisions take too long
	Committee structure time consuming
	Lack of agreed direction
	Lack of consistency of approach
Adequate IT systems	Lack of computer skills
	Dependence on outside IT support
OPPORTUNITIES	THREATS
Local connections	Fees overall being driven down
Wide range of services	Increased competition from other firms
Specialist services	Increased pressure on traditional fee areas
Diversification into non-professional areas	Increasing complexity of work
	Increased competition from non-professional sources

It is not untypical for the SWOT exercise to produce more weaknesses and threats. People are often overloaded and focus on the negatives rather than the positives. If that happens, it is important to encourage people to come up with more strengths! Sometimes, staff and clients will be able to do that better than the partners!

4.4.1 Strengths and weaknesses

For most professional service organisations, many of the strengths and weaknesses stem from people, as their contribution is essential to the provision of a quality service. The largest cheque any people-based organisation writes every month is for its salary bill. This investment needs to be maximised by making people feel valued for their contribution. In return, they will work hard for the organisation. Firms need their commitment, not only to make the best use of this expenditure, but also to harness the added value that the market place now demands from its professional service firms.

4.4.2 Opportunities and threats

In general terms, the opportunities and threats are common to other professionals working in the same market place. Except for the largest professional firms and multinationals, individual firms have limited control over their external environment. To some extent, this is in the hands of their professional bodies within whose constraints they have to operate. This reinforces the role that these bodies have in influencing the market place and clients' attitudes in general. This lack of individual control or influence means that within each profession, all firms may well be working within the same growth and development options. This has the effect of limiting their responses, especially when the market is overcrowded. We will consider the external market place and its effect in more detail in Chapter 6. The focus in this chapter is on providing internal, rather than external, solutions.

Having completed this SWOT exercise, the results need to be collated and discussed by as many people as possible. It may have already identified some key actions that need to be taken to address any weaknesses. For example, from the suggested SWOT, outlined in Table 4.1, the firm needs to make its clients more aware of the range of expertise and services offered. In addition, IT training is a priority to help with current work levels and reduce dependence on external IT support.

As explained at the outset, everyone – partners, staff, clients and contacts – needs to contribute to the future success of the organisation. It is essential to continue to involve them and build on their commitment.

4.5 The resource audit

The next phase is to complete a resource audit of the organisation, which is not as hard to do as it may sound. Basic information may already exist in the way of management accounts, performance- and client-management systems. Once the initial groundwork has been done, information then only needs to be updated for future reviews. People will also become more informed and, as a result, more knowledgeable. This will assist in future discussions and facilitate the implementation of current priorities.

All of the resources need to be examined in some detail to establish the current capabilities of the organisation. The following highlights the areas that should be considered (see the audit checklist Table 4.2).

4.5.1 People

As illustrated in the SWOT analysis in Table 4.1, people are crucial to the success or failure of professional service organisations. Not only do we need their direct input into our service delivery, but often the only distinguishing feature between service providers from the client perspective is the personal relationship that develops. Every organisation should identify its unique strengths in this area. One of the most useful sources of that information will be clients themselves (see later examples of how to obtain this in Chapter 5).

Questions should be asked to establish how effectively people are working, what areas are causing internal frustration or a lack of service support, where there are areas of over- or undercapacity. In addition, department performance and interdepartmental communications should be looked at. Traditional human-resource tools such as training needs analysis, job roles and performance reviews can be adapted to suit the needs of the organisation, supplemented by questionnaires and/or one-to-one interviews. It is important to be careful about overloading staff in particular at this stage with questionnaires. Staff tend to assume the worst when audits are being carried out and, if so, will not contribute openly. It is essential therefore that, before starting, everyone is reassured about the purpose behind this exercise to establish that this is a real opportunity to make the organisation better from everyone's point of view. This reflects the importance of open communications discussed in Section 3.5.2. Direct face-to-face discussions are more valuable than memos or e-mails!

Professionals are often very resistant to any kind of audit of their work practices or competence. I remember the first time my management team "appraised" me. I have rarely felt so insulted that my peers were passing comments on my performance, and looking back I was probably less than helpful as a result! This reinforces the comments that the managers of the organisation need to inspire the trust and respect of everyone. The only basis to achieve a positive outcome from this exercise is to go back to the core values of both the individual and the organisation.

4.5.1.1 Skills audit

A traditional HR technique is to carry out a skills audit on an organisation, which usually works on the assumption that people are clear about their roles and responsibilities. Given the lack of formal structure typical of most professional

Table 4.2 Audit checklist

1 People issues

- how effectively are individuals working?
- how effectively are departments working?
- how effective is cross-department support?
- do we have excess capacity?
- do we have areas under pressure?
- is training required?

2 Finance

- how quickly is up-to-date information produced?
- how accessible is it?
- how accurate is our working-capital information?
- how effective is our debt recovery?
- what is causing late/non-payment of fees?
- what are our current levels of work in progress?
- how recoverable are they?
- are we seeking payments to account?
- are we seeking early payment of outlays?
- how consistent are our recovery procedures?
- how will we fund future capital purchases?

3 Pricing and service-level issues

- what is our feeing policy?
- are we feeing at profitable levels?
- on what basis are we setting fees – e.g. cost to us, based on what clients will pay or as a response to the levels set by our competitors?
- what are the profitable areas of our business?
- what are our current service levels?
- should we be outsourcing areas of work?

4 Supplier issues

- are we purchasing effectively?
- how can we eliminate excess usage/wastage?
- are our leasing arrangements cost effective?

5 Administration and systems

- who is responsible for making decisions about administration?
- do we need all the office space we are currently occupying?
- do we have the right equipment in the right places?
- do we have the correct software packages?
- are people using them fully?
- are we too dependent on external IT support?

6 Client base

- why do our clients come to us?
- why do our clients stay with us?
- why have clients left us?

(*continued*)

Table 4.2 (cont.)

- where do we have expertise?
- what are we known for?
- which clients are profitable?
- do we have the right mix of services?

7 Quality
- how do our clients define the quality of our service?
- what elements add value to them?
- what elements do they take for granted?
- what external benchmarks can we develop?

8 Competitors
- who are our direct competitors?
- who are our indirect competitors?
- how well do we compare on price, location, range and quality of services?
- how can we effectively compete with them?
- how can we make adjustments to these areas to improve our competitive position?

partnerships, this is not always easy to achieve. Any skills audit may therefore have to be pre-dated by asking people to write down what they think their role in the organisation is, what expertise they have and how they think they could be better used. It is also worthwhile asking the partners what they think their role is! Some will favour business getting, others business doing, others training young people, others leading by example. No two partners are likely to be the same. This always produces fascinating results, with individuals tending to emphasise the importance of what they enjoy doing and/or are good at!

All firms should be able to develop a picture of what a "good partner" would look like. Most will include technical and client skills, business and financial awareness and the like, but each will have its own emphasis on the individual elements (or weighting of them) which make up their "good partner". This picture can be adapted for the role of "associate partner", which will illustrate the differences between that role and that of partner, helping career progression.

A similar exercise can be completed for any number of roles within the organisation, building up a generic picture of the key skills and knowledge needed by the firm. This can then be used in conjunction with other people audits, such as performance reviews, to identify gaps and/or underutilisation.

4.5.1.2 Performance reviews

As outlined above, there are a number of HR tools which can be used to carry out a review of people and their skills. Any appraisal or review processes should be adjusted to suit the firm. I am personally against a formal scoring system and prefer the use of open questions, as it is difficult to quantify a good professional.

A good professional must be able to use his/her judgement in a number of areas to respond to the needs of individual clients. Some pieces of work go well because the problem is straightforward, others are not and may take longer to complete. Some may go badly through no lack of skill on the part of the professional. As a result, it is very difficult to score people on the basis of client successes alone. Using the picture of "good partner" or "good associate" allows a wider evaluation of people's performance. It is often more useful to focus on the positive, rather than the negative – to ask what went well over the year, and what has been learned from what did not go well.

In addition, the line manager who works directly with the member of staff should carry out the review. This is preferable to having it conducted by someone who does not have direct experience of that individual's performance and has to rely on second-hand opinions. Again, this reinforces the importance of having hard data about the firm. Time recording can provide useful information about people's workloads and efficiency.

One area that needs careful thought is the link between any performance-review discussion and follow-up action. It is frustrating to take the time to prepare for and have these sessions, when no follow-up occurs. People must see a direct value in the exercise, otherwise they will begin to pay lip service to it. This highlights another area where partnerships will differ from other organisations. In most other types of organisations, the manager conducting the review will have the authority to agree any follow-up action or support. In professional firms, this may not be the case. If the firm operates in such a way that all the partners require to agree to such action or support, then the process must allow any options to be debated *prior* to the formal review discussion. Otherwise, that discussion involves two sessions – one to identify the options and then, after agreement with the partners, the follow-up action. This is cumbersome and takes up too much time.

I would therefore recommend that the member of staff completes a pre-review form, which will include the identification of what development support is being sought. This should be submitted to the partner/manager in sufficient time before the formal review discussion to allow the partners to meet and agree what support will be provided. All the forms should be discussed at the same time, which allows a holistic approach to be taken to the development of the firm. The partner/manager can then agree this with the member of staff during their session, as well as pointing out the link to the overall plan of the firm, thus reinforcing the contribution that the individual makes to the firm as a whole.

For professional firms in particular, with traditional fee areas under pressure, it is vital to identify whether there is scope to increase delegation to a more cost-effective level. There will often be areas of skills and/or expertise not fully utilised which can be developed or enhanced. Again, the process of performance reviews allows a discussion of such options. Using open questions is important; for example, asking where the member of staff sees himself/herself in 2 years' time. This encourages the member of staff to think longer term and much wider than his/her current role.

Reception is often an area with surplus capacity and expertise. For example, many receptionists are ideally qualified to take on responsibility for client data management. Most professional firms realise the importance of accurate information on clients, yet many of them never seem to get around to getting it onto the computer. Receptionists will already be familiar with many of the clients, their names and personal information, and will be happy to take responsibility for database management. Putting a PC on their desk allows them to work on this in quieter periods of their day. It also ensures that the information is accurate, up-to-date and personalised!

4.5.2 *Finance*

Many organisations will have good financial information, with detailed printouts circulated every month. What is important is that the financial information is accessible, up to date and understandable!

Basic management information should be available as a matter of routine. However, this should be tailored to the needs of the organisation as too much and/or irrelevant information can be damaging. It can confuse and exhaust the diligent professional manager and exasperate the unwilling. The information provided should be clear enough to allow informed decisions to be made at *the time that they need to be made.*

People need to be aware of current financial information. Some may need training to achieve a better understanding of financial management and what that entails. Most professionals, other than accountants, have had a very limited exposure to this in their professional training and are therefore uncomfortable with it. We tend to shy away from what is unfamiliar to us. This resistance must be overcome so that people can talk about these issues in an informed way. Rather than complain about the uselessness of such data, they should be asked to identify areas where clearer targets need to be established to measure future effectiveness. Be warned, however – professionals learn quickly. Many financial managers have faced problems when their professionals not only understand the basis of financial information but, as a result, challenge some of the assumptions. Clinical directors have been known to question the validity of bed-occupancy figures as a basis of allocating overheads, when long-stay geriatric departments bear higher charges than intensive-care units!

If based on accurate assumptions, these figures can provide useful information for current and future decisions. For example, one department of a law firm I worked with was alleged to be a cost centre. This was mostly based on the opinion of one of the senior partners, who happened to work in another department! When costs were properly allocated, it was found that the department in question contributed regular and positive cash flow to the firm. The partners in that department worked as a team providing cover for each other when needed. As a result, they were providing a cost-effective service with considerable flexibility. However, they were overloaded in one area, with client services under pressure. On the basis of this accurate financial information, the firm made the decision to invest in computer software to support that type of work, allowing partners to delegate to para-professionals. Not only did this get rid of the bottleneck of current work, it allowed the firm to target more of this type of work, thus increasing the fee income and making that department even more profitable. It also helped the confidence levels of these partners in further discussion with the senior partner!

The finance audit should include break-even calculations which help to illustrate the importance of fixed and variable overheads. Analysis of working capital, debt recovery, outlays and work in progress improve people's understanding of cash flow and efficient management of money. Work in progress, in particular, can provide useful information about the future cash flow of the firm. Investigation of the reasons behind late payment or non-payment of fees often offers information on client satisfaction and client relations. It can also track the effectiveness of the firm's feeing policy. As outlined in Chapter 3, establishing a feeing policy up front with clients is essential, both from the point of view of developing good client relations and to allow effective management of the firm.

One of the most common problems centres on cash-flow management. Traditionally fees in established professional firms were paid almost by default at the end of the transaction. Filing cabinets contained months of work in progress which provided a cushion for any slack periods. With increased pressure on fee levels in the early 1990s, firms saw this potential and started to fee on an interim basis. Whilst that provided a short-term solution for a few months or even a year, it resulted in firms being much leaner and much more susceptible to downturns in workloads. Interim fees are important to ensure that the firm is not lying out time and work in progress. Most clients prefer to know on a regular basis how much their advisers are costing them.

Professionals working in not-for-profit or government-funded organisations are being asked to become more accountable. Few professionals in these sectors have had formal training in accounting or budget holding. They may also feel that this emphasis on finance as a key driver of decisions is against their professional values. As a result, they will often challenge the validity or relevance of this type of information and block any attempts to identify and monitor targets. It is important to accept and address this. It reflects the importance of resolving this perceived dichotomy between professional and commercial as soon as it occurs. Managers should offer training in financial management for those directly affected or provide professionals with support from other professionals expert in these areas.

Checking against industry norms is also useful in allowing a comparison of the firm's performance against others. The professional bodies often offer good information in this area (for more information on this and on financial management in general see Otterburn, 1998a, b).

4.5.3 Pricing and service levels

Analysis needs to be done around current fee levels and what they are based on. They may reflect historical data which is now out of date, or what are perceived to be the market level. Many firms in the early 1990s dropped fee levels for traditional areas of work because of a decline in work because of the economic recession. Some firms managed this by changing work practices, substituting increased use of technology for expensive professional input. However, other firms dropped their fees without changing the way that they worked, with the result that their professionals were forced to work harder and harder for less return. These firms saw what the market was doing but failed to appreciate what they needed to do to respond.

4.5.3.1 *Time is money*

One of the most important aspects of any audit of a professional service firm is an analysis of its use of time. Time quite literally is money as many firms charge on a time-spent/time-recovered basis. Even where firms are working to fixed and/or success fees, it is still essential to know how much time has been spent on a particular matter and how much was recovered. This then allows decisions to be taken about how that work can be better managed.

It is essential that a full analysis of profit levels be carried out to establish the actual cost of the work. Indeed, partners may not be charging the same as each other for the same or similar work! One of the best systems my private practice firm introduced to address this was that every fee note had to be signed off by another partner before being accepted by the cash room. Attached to it was a copy of the current work-in-progress printout generated by our computerised accounting system. If the fee was less than the cost to the firm, this had to be explained and justified. Whilst it was rare that partners disagreed over the eventual fee, it was a good discipline to ensure not only that the work was undertaken as efficiently as possible, but that the fee was fair to both the client and the firm. It also led to some interesting discussions and trade-offs!

This analysis of profit levels again is not a difficult exercise and should not become a mammoth number-generating task. Many firms have computerised time-recording systems which produce the information as a matter of routine. This provides a great deal of valuable information, not only about the profitability of different areas of work, but also the working-style preferences of the fee earners, with some people spending all day on the phone, others in meetings! It illustrates what a routine client case involves and costs the firm to deliver. The cost of installing any time-recording system will be quickly recovered if the information it provides is used to adjust fee levels or work practices.

Even without such a computerised system, samples of files can be looked at to estimate the actual cost against the recovered fee. Basic stages of transactions can be identified and compared, which allows the firm to have a better understanding of what work is profitable and what is not. Too often firms confuse being busy with being profitable.

Another area that should be considered is the level of service being provided. As we have already discussed, professionals often prefer their definition of quality of service to that required by the client. This should be investigated to ensure that what the firm provides matches clients' expectations. For example, one accountancy firm confused speed of response with quality of service. One client commented that he did not appreciate being sent photocopies of the other side's correspondence, without any input from the professional. The professional, on the other hand, had felt it important to get the correspondence out to the client as soon as it came in, rather than wait until he had a chance to consider it. As the client pointed out, he was not paying the professional to be a photocopier – he was paying him for his advice!

A final aspect of pricing and service levels involves the consideration of the use of subcontractors or outsourcing. Given the current erosion of traditional areas of fee income, most firms are having to give consideration to whether, given the profitability of certain areas of work, it should be kept. One option is to outsource it. A number of the big corporations and some elements of the public sector have adopted this route. The organisation may already be subcontracting certain aspects or areas of its services. Again this requires careful analysis to ensure that it is cost effective.

4.5.4 Suppliers

The next area to consider is current supplier sources and costs. This requires analysis of what is being bought in, how often and at what cost. Savings can often be made with better sourcing and timing.

The actual use of these supplies should be considered. People get into the habit of using materials without any consideration of the actual cost. Staff often observe areas of wastage or excess usage but feel it is not their place to comment. Setting up small project teams involving cross-sections of the organisations can be tasked to carry out this element of the analysis and identify areas of inefficiency. These teams can continue to monitor usage and agree targets to be achieved.

Both purchase and leasing arrangements should be considered. However, it is important not to allow partners and senior managers to get bogged down in too much detail. As already explored, professionals have a marked preference for interfering in areas of administration!

One of the most contentious areas for any partnership is the question of partners' cars. Many partnership meetings have discussed the issues of leasing or owning and/or whether associate partners should be included. I have no solution to this debate other than to point out that it often takes up hours of valuable time which could be much better used!

4.5.5 Administration and systems

Analysing people's use of time will have identified areas of inefficiencies in the support systems. This will include not just work being done at the wrong professional level, but work being done by the wrong people. For example, some partners "tinker" in IT and can spend hours playing with system problems instead of leaving it to the professional IT manager!

On the wider administration front, an audit should be made of current use of office space and equipment. The system audit should include communications, information access and the firm's use of technology. The development of IT, and the option of working out of the office that this allows, offers the potential to reduce fixed overheads, such as office accommodation. The pattern of work has also changed with clients wanting 24-hour access to their professionals. People are seeking more flexibility in their own approach to work. Firms need to carefully consider the impact of any change in work practices on the firm and on individuals. Potential cost savings on property leases have to be set against the cost of computer hardware and communication support. People skills will also have to be adjusted to support a less cohesive approach to service delivery. Again, the values of the firm must be considered. For example, if the firm places a high value on teamworking, how will it ensure that this continues to be achieved if people start working from home?

Practical aspects should be considered, such as the siting of photocopiers and files. Moving the cash room from the basement to the middle of the office can reduce time spent running up and down stairs! Having too many photocopiers which become too easily accessible can increase photocopying costs. Similarly, inconveniently sited equipment can reduce working efficiency. Given the increased dependence on computerisation, this is an area where resources can be wasted or generate considerable savings. A current topical issue is the use of e-mail and the time spent generating, reading and discarding messages! This whole area merits dedicated and continued attention. In addition, the needs for current and future capital expenditure should be considered.

4.5.6 Client base

It is also important at this stage to analyse the current client base. This information should be easily accessible and up to date. If this is not the case, it should become a priority. Resistance from partners should be ignored and client information accessed from whatever sources are available. Basic client-information systems should be introduced and monitored. Modern accounting software often integrates core information which facilitates updating of the data. Partners should then be asked to confirm the accuracy of the data.

One of the key pieces of information that should be obtained from new clients is why they have come to the organisation. This is invaluable information on a number of fronts as it identifies:

- the perceived strengths of the organisation;
- the referral sources which need to be developed;
- what makes the firm "unique" in the eyes of that client; and
- what made the client "buy" the firm?

It also allows the organisation to check the demand for future services and its potential for growth in these areas. These should then be invested in and developed.

The range of products and services provided should also be analysed. One of the models frequently used to facilitate this is the Boston Consultancy Group model (Henderson, 1970, Table 4.3).

Table 4.3 Relative market share in market segment		
	High growth High market share	High growth Low market share
Growth rate of	Stars	Question Marks
	Low growth High market share	Low growth Low market share
Market segment	Cash Cows	Dogs

This encourages organisations to sort their current products or services into those which are making money for the business and those which are not. It also emphasises the need to constantly develop new products and services as the market does not stand still. Most organisations need a mix of Cash Cows (i.e. work that they can easily manage and produce without too much effort or investment), and Stars, which involve a higher level of investment and effort, but provide a higher rate of return. Dogs, which are not profitable, should be abandoned. There should always be a series of Question Marks currently under development which will provide the Stars and Cash Cows of the future.

This powerfully illustrates some of the problems currently facing professional firms. Too many of their traditional Cash Cows (audit, conveyancing, executry/ probate, etc.) have moved into Dogs. Too many firms are fighting over the Stars (commercial deals) and too few firms have replaced their Cash Cows!

Regular checks should be made with existing clients and contacts as to current levels of service, which is best achieved through direct discussions, rather than written questionnaires. This is developed in more detail in Chapter 5. Analysis of the clients themselves is important. We often work with clients who in real terms cost us money. For good or bad reasons, they absorb a great deal of time with limited return. We will look at saying no to these types of clients in Section 5.8, but it is important that *we have the data* on which to base these decisions. Analysis is therefore required to ascertain which clients should be encouraged and which discouraged.

4.5.7 Quality

The next area, and perhaps the most subjective, is an analysis of the quality of the service provided. Many firms will talk about delivering a quality service without any real idea of what that involves. Others will produce an aim which states that they "intend to improve the quality of their service year on year" again without any mechanism of measuring the current level! There are a number of external quality initiatives which firms can use to benchmark the quality of their services. These currently include Investors in People, ISO 9000, Charter Mark, Lexcel and a number of National Training, European and World Class awards. Firms can also become members of network associations which often carry out internal audits.

However, even more importantly, firms need to appreciate that it is their clients, not them, who define the quality of their service. This requires a fundamental shift of emphasis and, once achieved, can provide vital data on what clients value and what they take for granted. This then allows firms to look at what they do and how. This can produce one of the main areas for cost reductions. For example, some clients do not want to be bothered with copies of documents. They want their professional to deal with all of this on their behalf. Others want to see every detail! Firms can make savings if they are aware of these preferences, subject to making sure that any audit trail or "back covering" is in place.

4.5.8 Competitors

Most professional firms are not well informed about their competitors and what they are doing. They will have access to a good deal of gossip and speculation, but little of this will be based on facts! Because of the tight networks within which their professionals have been trained, they will know many people working in other similar firms. Rumours abound with people talking confidentially and off the record. As most firms trade as partnerships, they do not need to publish their accounts, which makes it hard to distinguish between fact and fiction!

However, there are ways of accessing accurate and current data. Some firms are now publishing annual reports; the professional bodies promote "cost of time" surveys and the results of in-depth research with firms. Specialist-sector market analysis, such as Keynote Reports can be obtained, and the Internet provides access to a lot of hard data. All of this should be used as the basis of a "competitor analysis".

A formal analysis can be carried out to ascertain how well the firm is placed against its direct competitors. This should consider how well it competes on price, location and both the range and quality of product/service provided.

The following is a simple illustration of this. Firm X is a civil-engineering firm offering high-quality niche service to commercial clients. It has offices in both its major regional centres. It is not the cheapest but clients tell it that they choose it because it responds quickly to their needs. It has three direct competitors – Firms A, B and C. A and B are more expensive. B only operates in one centre. All three provide the same range of services but C has a poor reputation.

This information produces Table 4.4, where √ indicates that the firm performs better than its competitors.

Table 4.4				
	Price	Location	Range of services	Quality of services
Firm A	√			
Firm B	√	√		
Firm C				√

Adapted from Waterworth (1987, p. 152).

Table 4.4 allows the firm to see that if it promotes its good reputation, it can gain advantage over *C*. It can emphasise its lower price when competing with *A* and its price and location when competing with *B*. This allows the firm to "position" itself in the market place as well as identify areas where adjustments to pricing and/or location and/or services will make a real difference to the firm's share of the market.

This is a simple illustration of what can become a quite sophisticated analysis, which may involve "mystery shopper" visits to competitors!

4.6 First steps to success!

The above analysis can appear to be daunting to many firms. Some firms will have some of the information already and may only need to attack certain gap areas. Others may have a lot of data, but in a piecemeal and fragmented way. For example, they may have management information, but have not used it in terms of product/service mix. They may carry out performance reviews but do not link them to areas for potential increase in efficiency.

This project should not take longer than a couple of months, otherwise people lose impetus and get into too much detail. Parallel project teams can be set up, with the workload spread among partners and staff. Much of this information is essential for the future viability of the organisation and, as indicated before, it is important that decisions are made against hard data rather than by force of personality!

The firm now has a whole raft of information to work with. For example, it knows what areas of work are profitable and what are not. It knows which clients add value and which do not, what clients expect from the firm and where work can be delegated to a more profitable level. As far as possible, this data should be presented simply and kept up to date and accessible.

Decisions can now be taken on an informed basis. The information itself should not dictate the decision, but will facilitate an impersonal discussion of the options. These options will reflect the values of the firm, and may therefore require that some services be retained regardless of their profitability. For example, the firm may have overriding reasons why a client service will continue to be provided because, for example, it:

- provides a service to the community;
- services more profitable work;
- is a "lost leader" which helps to attract better paid work;
- is important for the firm's image and reputation; and/or
- is part of an overall strategy to develop specialist skills.

These are valid reasons and should not be disregarded because the figures indicate that they are not profitable in the short term.

The *process* of completing the analysis is as important as the information itself. By obtaining and working through the collation of information, people become more knowledgeable about the organisation as a whole, the detail of its operations and the interconnection of different elements. In addition, different groupings of people will have become more comfortable with working together and sharing views.

This segment of the Model is crucial as it provides some of the keys to "unsticking" accepted work practices and behaviours, and undermining ill-founded assumptions and attitudes. It is important to identify some key actions and put them into effect, which starts the firm on the road to success. This then builds the momentum and acceptance of change.

If not already available, proper management accounts should be generated as a matter of routine. The timing of these reports is important. They should be generated monthly rather than quarterly as quarterly reporting can result in firms looking at information which is perhaps 5 months out of date. Not only is it not likely to reflect the current situation, it is, by that time, too late to do anything about it! Also the discipline of producing the figures monthly means that they will have to be "short and sharp" (i.e. contain focused and relevant information).

Costs and overheads should be allocated to agreed areas of the organisation in such a way that people understand and accept these figures. Many professionals complain about the irrelevance of this type of information, often picking holes in these allocations to justify these assertions. This has to be addressed at this stage, with individual concerns identified and ironed out. Sometimes a compromise may have to be reached between financial accuracy and what is practicable.

What is essential is that the figures are used and used regularly. Many a firm carrying through this exercise has discovered significant cost reductions, as well as practical solutions to what were seen as "embedded problems".

Working from this base of knowledge, the organisation should then agree certain priorities and immediate actions, and develop an action plan. Priorities could include:

- training staff in IT, assertiveness and time management;
- reorganising staffing levels;
- reducing debtor days and outlays;
- reducing work-in-progress levels;
- improving fee recovery against work in progress;
- recruiting an IT manager;
- standardisation of routine documentation;
- completing the client database;
- investigating new areas of client services; and/or
- raising the firm's profile through increasing client contact.

The action plan must be specific about what needs to be done, what the outcomes will be, the timescales and people involved and any resource implications. Once agreed, it should be promulgated as widely as possible, with review dates adhered to. The tasks should be broken down into manageable chunks, which can be achieved within a short period of time, so that people feel that progress is being made. In addition, specific outcomes and/or critical success factors must be identified as otherwise no one will see the results of all this effort. Quick wins should be prioritised, achieved and communicated to everyone. It is absolutely essential that the timescales be adhered to. Progress reviews and updates should be completed every 2–3 months, with any reprioritising agreed.

Some of these actions may require restructuring or a reallocating of roles and areas of responsibilities. Others may require training. There may be certain drivers within the firm that are forcing the pace of change, such as the need to replace retiring partners or key personnel.

One of the most prevalent areas of pressure at the moment is the need to upgrade computer systems. This can offer the possibility of real improvements in efficiency and profitability. It can increase flexibility, quality, controls, integration and delegation. Most professional firms who have fully integrated computerisation describe achieving efficiency increases of at least 25%.

It is essential therefore that any investment in computers must be used! One firm described buying a debt-recovery system which lay on the shelf unopened for 3 years – by which time it was out of date! This investment must also include a *change in the way people work,* with work practices being reviewed at the same time. Otherwise, the financial investment will not be maximised and no real improvement in organisational performance achieved. Too often word processors become merely more expensive typewriters; or professionals with poor typing speeds are expected to generate their own paperwork. However, good examples do exist of improvements in both the cost and quality of work. Many architects have responded well to this opportunity and have fundamentally changed the profile of their staff to reflect this.

4.7 Learn to delegate

If clients ask what should be a priority for them, I would suggest that most professional firms could increase their efficiency considerably by improving their delegation. As indicated above, the impact of technology has produced the opportunity for a considerable change in the way that work is carried out. Building from what clients perceive as a quality service helps to indicate which areas of work can be streamlined and completed at a lower level. Analysis of profitable work will highlight areas where savings have to be made. People audits will have identified where people have the potential to take on new areas of responsibilities.

Delegation does not come easily to many professionals. They are by their nature independent and develop close relationships with their clients. They like to hoard their clients and their expertise! They therefore find it difficult to delegate, and can come up with a range of reasons for not doing so. These include:

- *it's easier and quicker to do it myself;*
- *no one understands the client like I do;*
- *people don't understand what I want;*
- *I can do it better than anyone else;*
- *the staff can't be trusted to work on their own;*

- *we are seriously understaffed;*
- *my work is in too much of a mess to hand it over; and*
- *I don't want to admit that I can't cope!*

All of these are excuses, rather than explanations. Managers will need to work with professionals and tease out the problems which lie behind. Professionals need to be encouraged to understand that they are not superhuman and may need help! It is important to work around their reasons for not doing it. For example, telling them that:

- *It will always be quicker to do it yourself – in the short term. But there will come a time when you collapse under the weight of responsibilities.*
- *No one will ever be able to understand what you want if you do not take the time to explain to people.*
- *If the firm is seriously understaffed then this has to be addressed.*

People working under too much pressure for sustained periods will become ineffective. They will become tired and will make mistakes. For professionals, making a mistake can be a major problem – for the firm, the client and the individual concerned!

We have already identified that time is money for professional service firms and has to be effectively managed, charged and recovered. Above all, *it should not be wasted.* The introduction of effective delegation is therefore one of the most important areas for any professional firm, and will provide real returns. Increasing investment in technology offers the potential to delegate well and effectively. It has become an invaluable tool to help deliver excellent client services cost effectively. The price of technology has reduced considerably with much of the software becoming user friendly to the most technophobic. Effective use can help us spend our time better, but it needs discipline to spend time in the short term to save time overall.

To delegate effectively takes time and patience – both of which are usually in short supply in professional firms. Managers should therefore start with the key areas of the firm where improving delegation will pay dividends and quickly, and/or where people seem most responsive to change. This will encourage other areas to look at the time invested and the returns achieved. As a result, they will become more sympathetic to suggestions that they need to change the way that they work. We identified before the savings that were made by the law firm whose department was overloaded in one area of their client work. By introducing software and delegating to para-professionals, the department quickly became less pressured and more profitable. This resulted in other departments in that firm being much more responsive to the introduction of IT to change the way that they worked!

As indicated above, managers will need to convince people that taking time now will produce dividends – *financially, professionally and personally.*

Start by looking at every element of what people do. Ask yourself whether it needs to be done at all! If the answer is yes, is the best person doing it, or given training, is there someone else that can do it more effectively? It is important to look at every aspect of what we do because we can get into bad habits and/or do what we are comfortable with and/or use routine work to put off doing more difficult work. It is often easier for an outsider or someone from another area of the firm to challenge some of the assumptions that we routinely make about how we work and why. The support staff in particular will be well able to focus on where professionals are wasting time and energy!

Everyone can adopt bad habits and waste time without being aware of it. The people audit will have identified some key areas where people are willing to take on more work.

4.7.1 People are willing to take on more!

Most research indicates that most people want to have interesting jobs. They are prepared to learn new skills and take on more responsibility, if they are allowed to learn and get recognition for what they do. To delegate effectively therefore requires the establishment of clear expectations on both sides. The development of computerisation offers the potential not only to move support staff through to para-professionals, but also provides the mechanism to set clear standards for the firm to work to.

The skills for effective delegation are similar to those required for effective management. They therefore include the ability to plan, organise, motivate and control. Key issues are:

- what do both parties want to get out of this? (planning);
- what additional support is needed? (i.e. physical resources, formal and informal training, coaching and advice) (organising);
- what motivates that individual? (i.e. money, security, fellowship, challenge and how can these be maximised) (motivating);
- what timescales are involved and how can success be reviewed and measured? (controlling).

In all cases, delegation is not abdication. People must be allowed to learn – that implies that they may make mistakes! The firm must be tolerant of these, but use the control mechanism to insist that managers take responsibility for picking errors up at an early stage and resolve them. People should be given feedback – both positive and negative – as a matter of routine. This should be built in to any formal performance review.

Delegation also means that people are coping with change. Establishing some structure can help to address that. For example, agreeing roles and responsibilities for people allows them to not only identify their contribution to the firm and its overall success but also provides a framework within which to delegate. It also clarifies individual responsibility for certain key tasks, providing reinforcement of that level of authority when dealing with others. People cannot then "duck" responsibility for what they have been asked to do and other people cannot overtly interfere.

Behind-the-scenes resistance can also be a major problem, especially in partner-ships where there are many "chiefs". Accepting that change can cause stress means that people can be more open about how they are feeling. Offering training in stress management or "working under pressure" is one way of tackling this. Another way is to refer back to the value discussions referred to in Chapter 3. If people feel that their values are not being threatened and that any change will respect these, they will be less likely to block and resist it.

Once people have evidence that they are being *supported* to learn and adapt, then they will become comfortable with taking on more responsibilities. As long as they trust the people who are managing their learning and feel that they are being openly communicated with, and as long as their values continue to be met, then they will respond positively to what is being asked of them.

4.8 Areas that hijack our time

We all need to notice the habits that our organisation has developed! Some firms are very "collegiate", with people in and out of other people's offices all of the time. Others can be very calm and tranquil. An analysis of how people spend their time will throw up areas where the firm is losing time and therefore money.

Mail opening causes a lot of debate within firms, as it can take up a good deal of time. Some prefer for all the partners to be involved, others to leave it to reception or the cash room. Some emphasise the importance of having everyone involved, so that people can have the opportunity of seeing what is going on. This argument is becoming less relevant with increasing use of faxes and e-mails!

"Black files" are another problem area. We all have files which through no fault of anyone "go wrong". They become a *bête noire* with people unable to bring themselves to look at them, even yet open them. The firm should set up a system which allows people to swap their black file with someone else. It is much easier and quicker to sort out someone else's problems than your own. Swapping means that both parties benefit and neither feels guilty about asking for help. It also saves a lot of time and subsequent client and professional complaints.

Research indicates that we take much longer to complete tasks we do not like doing! It is important to encourage people (through the people audit) to identify what they hate doing and swap it for something they enjoy. For example, if a partner hates feeing, rather than spend endless management time trying to persuade him/her to do it, he or she should swap it with someone who likes feeing and get him/her to do something for them in return. This will save a lot of time and energy!

Another main area which hijacks time is the amount spent in meetings. Too often people get into bad habits about meetings. Meetings are arranged without thinking through what they are to achieve and/or whether they are the best way to progress matters. Where people have too many routine meetings, they develop "meeting inertia" with no expectation of achieving or resolving anything!

People should be encouraged to consider whether calling a meeting would be a good use of time. Do we really need a meeting to progress the matter? If so, what is its purpose, who needs to be there and will all the necessary information be available on time?

Anyone responsible for calling a meeting should be encouraged to carry out a "meeting audit" which looks at, for example:

- what kind of meeting is it? (i.e. to inform people, to discuss issues and/or to make a decision)
- who *needs* to be at the meeting?
- are people clear about its purpose, duration and anticipated outcomes?
- will all the information be available in sufficient time for people to be up to speed to make the best use of the time spent in the meeting?
- if a decision is needed, do people have the authority to make a decision?

We should always make sure that follow-up action is agreed, allocating individual responsibilities and timescales.

If people need any incentive to carry out this exercise, suggest that the next time they are in a meeting, which is taking up their valuable time, they work out the combined hourly rates of the people round the table and see if its outcomes are cost effective!

CONCLUSIONS

Working through this segment of the Model allows firms to analyse their current resource base and develop their management skills. It also identifies the financial systems and people resources that are needed for the future as well as providing hard data on the strengths of the organisation and its weaknesses. As a result, it can identify areas which are performing well and other areas which need additional support.

By achieving steady and incremental change, the organisation develops its ability to change. Underpinned by accurate data, improved skills, knowledge and understanding, active involvement, open communications and sharing of information, it achieves a forward momentum.

By consolidating the resource base, eliminating wastage and duplication, and ensuring effective work practices, the firm has a sounder foundation for future growth. All of this will allow it to develop its plans for the future and, most important of all, implement them.

 ## *KEY ACTION POINTS*

➢ Be aware of the strengths and weaknesses of the organisation

➢ Tackle sensitive issues such as current and future workloads

➢ Don't let issues fester

➢ Make sure that the firm has accurate hard data and facts

➢ Audit all resources – both hard and soft

> Involve as many people as possible

> Time is money – manage and recover it effectively

> Train people in financial awareness

> Render interim fees

> Know where the firm is better than its competitors

> Make sure that the firm has a strong service mix

> Know why clients come to the firm and stay with it

> Maximise any investment in IT by making sure that people change the way that they work

> Delegate to the most effective level possible

> Don't just analyse – identify key priorities and implement them

> Promote successes and savings achieved

> Watch areas which hijack people's time

> Make sure all meetings are necessary and effective.

5. Improving Our Client Focus

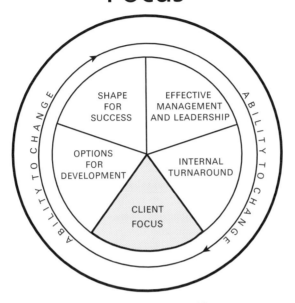

THE MODEL FOR SUCCESS

5.1 Introduction

This segment of the Model looks at the importance of adopting and maintaining a client focus. Historically, professionals were criticised for a lack of client awareness – for not being accessible, of running their organisations to suit themselves rather than their clients. It used to be possible for professionals to set their own time-tables for workloads, with clients prepared to wait for a "considered response". This was true of both the private and public sector. More recently, however, increased competition in both sectors has encouraged them to become more "client focused".

Professionals now complain of a lack of client loyalty, with clients shopping around for the "best deal". Clients have become more demanding, no longer prepared to wait for consultations and appointments. Client work itself has become more complex and technical, with numerous changes in rules and regulations every year. The introduction of faxes and e-mail has meant that response times have been reduced. Many professionals currently work long hours with limited control over their working days and weeks. Symptoms of stress and overwork are now common. This chapter will consider the implications of all of this.

We have to be responsive to clients but, at the same time, be able to take some control over our working week. One traditional area of complaint is that professionals are poor communicators. Another focuses around fees and what professionals charge. This chapter will look at both of these and offer some suggestions to improve client relations in general.

5.2 The background

Most professionals have in the past been criticised for their lack of client focus. Too often, surveyors and lawyers were hard to get hold of, doctors impregnable behind their protecting receptionists, dentists seemingly clinical and impersonal, accountants focusing on the figures rather than the person.

Many professional firms closed for lunch, were not open after 5 p.m. and certainly not at weekends! Professionals were used to having their judgement accepted without question. They responded to clients' demands at a pace which suited them. The technical nature of the job was fairly stable and based on learning established at university and in early training. It was therefore easy to keep up to date. Life was pleasant and rewarding!

During the 1970s and early 1980s fees were sent out (and paid!) every month without too much attention being paid to cash flow and overheads. A comfortable lifestyle was assured for those in their forties and fifties who had made partner. Young professionals were happy to work hard and carry out routine work with the carrot of partnership and that lifestyle encouraging them on.

However, during the mid- to late 1980s, all professional life became more complex. The development of technology demanded new skills and ways of working, as well as investment in more sophisticated equipment. The significant increase in legislation and regulations made it much more difficult to keep up to date. As a result, people became more specialised, narrowing their focus to maintain expertise. To cope with this pressure on resources, organisations often merged to achieve economies of scale and/or provide a pool of skills. As a result, clients were passed between professionals to ensure that the most competent person dealt with their problem.

In the 1990s, with the economy depressed, firms were competing for a reducing base of business. At the same time, scale fees were abolished, which resulted in downward pressure on fees in general as firms sought to attract enough work to remain profitable. Indirect competition increased with architects seeing surveyors chase their work, with accountants stepping into areas traditionally the domain of the lawyers. Many firms were under extreme pressure, with the banks even declaring that professional firms were on their "at risk" category. Tensions within partnerships increased with cracks appearing in people's relationships. Partners left and formed new and/or smaller firms.

The market place became increasingly overcrowded as a result. In addition, universities continued to produce graduates who had difficulty finding professional training. With pressure on profits, people were reluctant to recruit and invest in young people, which resulted in a lack of investment in quality professionals for the future. Good professionals saw little opportunity to develop within firms struggling with cash flow. Partners were reluctant to delegate protecting *their* clients from other people, sometimes tackling work that they were ill-equipped to do despite the pressure to specialise as work became more complex. People had little time or energy to keep up to date. Mistakes were made as a result of pressure of work or ignorance. This in turn increased tensions within firms and externally with clients.

Clients started to move around more. It became more acceptable to do this as firms were keen to attract new clients, regardless of why they had left their previous advisers. Professionals could no longer assume the loyalty of existing clients, observing this "promiscuity" with increasing horror! (As an aside, it seems odd that professionals describe this behaviour as promiscuous, whilst at the same time, seeing no issue with talking to a number of car dealerships to get the best price for a new car!)

To respond to all of this, professionals were encouraged to develop and improve client relationships. Many management books (and rightly so), advocated the importance of "delighting the customer" (Peters and Waterman, 1982 as well as Peters and Austin, 1985 were influential in this field, and both books contain good advice). Many firms improved their image by developing brochures, upgrading their offices and investing in marketing expertise. Professionals accepted that they had no control over their days – that they had to be totally responsive to client demands; to compete they had to deliver whatever the client wanted and whenever.

All of this has resulted in increased workloads. Many partners in their forties and fifties say that they are now working harder than they have ever done – and certainly did not expect to be working this hard at this stage of their professional life! All professionals are now used to working under pressure, but these levels of activity have become prolonged, and in many cases are not sustainable. People are looking tired and drawn. Some are exhibiting signs of severe stress, such as health problems and burn-out.

5.3 Why is having a client focus important?

We have considered in earlier chapters the importance of providing a high-quality professional service. This is the minimum clients expect from us and rightly so. They are paying us for our professional judgement and expertise – to listen to their needs and respond to them. For our part, no professional would disagree with that premiss. We care about our clients and the services we render.

However, one fundamental change of focus is required before we proceed with the rest of this discussion. It is *the client* who is the judge of the level of our service, not us! This is often very difficult for firms to appreciate. They will talk a great deal about the importance of being client focused, but by that they mean delivering the level of service and/or type of services that *they think* the client wants. However, to be truly client focused requires the firm first to investigate and then deliver what the client defines as a high-quality professional service. This means that firms have to understand and respect their clients.

Once this mind shift has been achieved, it is much easier to develop client-focused services and *measure the effectiveness of them.*

This leads into the vexed area of client-satisfaction questionnaires and surveys. Most professionals are reluctant to "open the box" of asking clients what they think of their service. Some send out satisfaction questionnaires at the end of a file, asking for comments about basic services, such as how quickly the phones are answered. These often provide limited responses and even more limited useful data. What is important is to ask clients more open questions about what they think of the services provided (e.g. in terms of timeliness and/or value for money).

Rather than using questionnaires, where the answers are often difficult to interpret and may pose more questions than they answer, firms should speak directly to certain key clients/groups of clients. This can be done informally at the end of a routine meeting and/or over lunch, or can be carried out more formally through end-of-project reviews. It can also be achieved through focus groups and/or involving clients in strategy discussions. This level of sophistication depends on the size of the firm and/or the clients.

In addition, it is important to check out with them what the firm has identified as its strengths and/or its weaknesses, as this may highlight other issues. Another important element is to ask them what services they will want in the future, how they would want these provided and by whom. This will provide important information about the future strategies for and shape of the firm. Table 5.1 poses these and other suggested questions in more detail. By their nature, these types of questions tend to be fairly blunt, which is another reason why it is easier to do this face to face with the client and work it into other more routine discussions. Some firms prefer to use external consultants to carry this through on their behalf, on the basis that clients may find it easier to speak to a third party. Whilst some clients may prefer not to speak directly with the firm, the disadvantage with this approach is that there is no opportunity for both sides to develop their existing personal relationship.

Despite initial reluctance, firms are often surprised about the amount of information that such sessions can provide, not only about current services, but also what the client will want from the firm in the future. Some have found out about fundamental concerns about personnel and/or response rates and/or costs. Others have identified the potential for new work which their clients had not been aware they could provide to them.

On a more general level, we cannot assume that we know what clients want from us. We need to ask them what services they want and how they want them to be delivered. This may require us to restructure our firms to match. For example, whilst a department/specialist structure might suit our areas of expertise and feeing policies, clients may not like dealing with a number of people within the firm and receiving fee notes charged on a different basis. Clients may prefer one point of contact and one rate of charge. Others, however, may be happy to use different levels of personnel for different work.

Table 5.1 The client audit

New clients
- What made you select our firm? (if by recommendation, get details)
- Have you moved professionals in the last 2 years?
- If yes, why did you move?
- What do you look for in a good professional?

Current clients and services
- Was the level of fee agreed with you before the work was started?
- Was it adhered to? If not, why not?
- Were timescales agreed?
- Were they adhered to? If not, why not?
- Did the project achieve what you expected?
- Did you feel that you received value for money? If not, why not?
- What went well?
- What could we have done better?
- Was there a sufficient level of face-to-face contact?
- Was there a sufficient level of communications?
- Were you comfortable with the level of information provided?
- What would you describe as the firm's strengths?
- What would you describe as the firm's weaknesses?
- How useful do you find our newsletter/brochure/website?

Future services
- In what areas do you anticipate your level of work with us will increase/decrease over the next 2 years?
- In what areas do you anticipate your level of work with us will increase/decrease over the next 5 years?
- What other areas will you be seeking professional support in the next 2–5 years?
- Where will you source them?
- How would you like these provided and by whom?
- Is the location of your professional important?
- To what extent would you want a one-stop shop?
- How would you define a "quality" professional service?
- What could professionals do better?

Some firms now accept the importance of continuing client contact by appointing "key client partners". This allows ongoing discussions about level of service delivery distinct from discussions about a particular piece of work. It also helps to maintain a client overview where a number of fee earners are working on different files.

5.4 Never assume client loyalty

Historically clients stayed with us unless something drastic happened. They were willing to accept a less than adequate service at times, without taking their business elsewhere. This is no longer the case. Client loyalty is a thing of the past. Clients are much more critical of their professionals and their advice. They are much more likely to question, or indeed, challenge our opinion, often seeking a second or outside confirmation. Whilst this is a reflection of increased consumerisation in general, clients are becoming more informed. Television programmes give commentary on a range of professional services, which also results in a demystifying of professional advice. In addition, new IT software allows clients to do some of the routine work themselves, which in turn educates them about the language used by professionals and how to question and challenge them.

Client loyalty therefore needs to be worked on – developed and nurtured, certainly not taken for granted. Contact must be maintained at all times. This can be achieved in a number of ways, for example, by:

- the use of client databases;
- the development of firm newsletters/updates;
- "not closing the file"; and
- becoming more involved in their organisations.

Whichever option is used must help to remind the client of the existence of the firm and its range of services, as well as reinforce the relationship in such a way that the client will think of us first rather than be tempted elsewhere.

The development of a *database* helps to maintain that contact, but organisations need to ensure that contact is maintained in an accurate and tailored way. Care has to be taken to make sure that the client data is up to date. There is nothing more annoying to a client to get a routine mailshot to the wrong address or addressed to an individual who has left the organisation or worse still died!

The development of *newsletters/updates* to clients can be another useful way of reminding clients of the firm's existence. They are also a way of building the profile of the firm. They can be costly – both in time and in their production. If developed, firms need to check with their clients how useful they find them. At a minimum, these publications should give clients information about the range of services provided by the firm and who to contact if they need advice.

Professionals are very guilty of "closing the file" on clients. Having finalised a piece of work, we are so relieved to have reached that stage that we want to close the file! To maintain client loyalty, we should not give this appearance. Instead we should keep in contact with the client personally, with updates and/or notes on changes that may affect them. We should appear to care about our clients and what is likely to concern them. Other options, which depend on the size and resources of the firm, can include secondment of professionals to client organisations. This is an extension of the more usual option of taking on official roles, such as company secretary or treasurer.

The overall aim of all of these activities is to blur the lines between the client and the professional, so that it becomes more difficult for them to shop around. For individual clients, we need to get to know them personally. For larger clients, the more we build ourselves into their teams and ways of working, the more we develop a "partnership" relationship with them.

5.5 Delighting the customer!

As explained above, many management gurus emphasise the importance of not just satisfying but "delighting the customer". None of us would disagree with this if we think how annoying it is to buy a new car and still have to pay for a full tank of petrol when we pick it up!

Yet, professionals often have to give clients information that they would rather not hear. Sometimes, we are dealing with clients who do not want to consult us in the first place. They have not chosen to select our services – but rather have been forced by circumstances or by the behaviour of others to seek our advice. Others see us as a necessary evil! Sometimes we cannot deliver the solution they want whether that is reassurance about a health problem or a successful resolution of their situation. What they want is simply not possible. We do not have a magic wand that will make everything right for them again. In addition, in most circumstances, we have to charge for our work, even if it provides no return to the client at all! In all of these circumstances it is impossible to "delight them". At best, by using all of our technical and interpersonal skills to the best of our ability, we may be able to provide the client with a solution which he/she can tolerate. At worst, despite doing our utmost for them, we will still be blamed for not delivering what they want.

We need therefore to be very careful about attempting to "delight our customers". What we do need to do is to provide a service which:

- delivers the best solution to the client at a fee which is acceptable to them; and at the same time
- allows delivery of a professional service at a price which is profitable to us.

That may require some readjustment of the client's expectations and a discussion about costs. Both of these should be tackled as early in the relationship as possible.

5.5.1 Step 1 Establish and agree client's expectations

Some professionals often shy away at the outset of a consultation to explain the pros and cons of the particular client situation, preferring to make vague assurances about likely outcomes. As a result, clients often come away with high expectations! It is important to remember that people have no real perception of what is involved in the service they are buying. Recent research with commercial organisations confirms this, describing the "leap of faith" which is required when instructing professionals. For example, most clients, when asking an architect to design a building, have no idea where his/her responsibility ends and that of other professionals and contractors begins.

Other professionals prefer to explain options and procedures in great detail. Clients then accuse them of putting obstacles in their way – of appearing negative and discouraging – of making things seem unnecessarily complicated! Sending out long terms-of-engagement letters, whilst necessary professionally, can appear to clients to be a back-covering exercise and a means of justifying an inflated fee.

Both approaches can create their own set of problems; but of the two approaches, the second (properly handled) is the preferred option if a good client relationship is to be developed and maintained. However, the explaining of options and procedures must be done sympathetically. Too often professionals, inured to the content of their work, forget how clients actually feel when they seek professional advice. Think how some people worry about visiting the doctor for a routine health check. Clients do not come to see professionals every day. Often, they are anxious about their situation and may have had to screw up their courage to contact us. They may be taking a huge risk with their future. Even the most hardened property-developer client will be under pressure at times. We must take the time to "settle" the client, to appreciate that they may be unhappy and worried and not assume that any prickliness is directed at us!

5.5.2 Step 2 Develop and retain trust

The essence of being client focused is based, from the outset, on our ability to develop and sustain trust. Once this has been established, the client relationship becomes much easier to manage. As explained above, we need to explain to the client the issues that will need to be handled, and the anticipated timescales and costs. It is important to be upfront with the client and deal with any unrealistic expectations that he/she has about what can realistically be achieved.

Increasing pressure on profits has caused many professionals to worry about putting clients off at the outset by explaining in detail what will be involved. The result is that clients leave early meetings with a sense of euphoria that the magic wand does exist and that everything will soon be rosy! Frustration then seeps in as more detailed information is required, time passes without apparently being any nearer a resolution, steps and stages appear which were not explained before. The client becomes disaffected, looking for sinister reasons in the delay – a lack of competence on the part of the professional, a way of milking fees and a sense of being "taken for a ride" – "of having the wool pulled over their eyes".

Even when the professional is following the normal path at the best speed possible, because the client was not alerted to this at the outset, client relations will become strained. On top of this, professionals are not good at being proactive in communicating with clients, preferring to wait until they have something positive to say. This can create a tension which is not healthy and, if things start to go wrong for any reason, can lead to strained relationships.

5.5.3 Step 3 Learn to listen

The next vital element is to make clients feel that we are "responsive" to their needs. As outlined in Section 5.5.1, we need to take time at the outset to "settle the client" – to listen to him/her and establish the basis of a working relationship. We should go though the same process we adopt when we delegate to people. We have to begin to understand what matters to that particular client and what motivates him/her. Many clients complain that we only appear to listen to what they are saying. This may be because we are already thinking through what the client is telling us and/or sorting through some alternatives in our head. The client is not aware of this and only sees us looking inattentive!

This is also an important stage from the marketing point of view. We know that the client has come to see us about the problem in hand. We should check why he/she has selected our firm and us in particular. Was it a personal recommendation? What was the source? This is important information for the firm, and helps to build up an action plan to attract future work. It is equally important at this stage to give the client information about the firm and all the services that it offers. We must not assume that clients know what we do. We may be able to distinguish between one type of surveying service and another, but not everyone can! We need to give them some background on the firm, its style and approach and what additional services it can provide. This can be backed up with promotional material, if appropriate.

It is also the opportunity to introduce the client to the concept that we are not accessible 24 hours every day. It is important to explain that there will be times when we cannot be interrupted (e.g. when in this meeting with him/her!). As a result of this, there will be times when the client will not be able to deal with us directly. It is important at this point to introduce them to the person *trusted* to deal with the client as we would do ourselves. The client must not feel that he/she is being fobbed off with second best!

5.6 Developing a good client relationship

Research (Nicou et al., 1994) indicates that there are a number of core factors that clients give priority to when choosing professional advisers. These include:

- professional or specialist knowledge;
- knowledge of the client's situation;
- accurate perception and empathy;
- analytical skills;
- results orientation;
- creativity;
- ethics and moral competence;
- communications skills;
- ability to co-operate; and
- integrity and courage.

Most of these relate to the "softer" aspects of client relationships rather than the "harder" technical skills and, surprisingly, fees are not amongst them. Corporate clients, in particular, identify the importance of tailoring the service to their needs, efficiency and timeliness of delivery, accessibility for discussions and availability of aftercare support (KPMG, 1994).

5.6.1 Settling the client

We need therefore to take the time to settle our clients. We need to create an understanding and rapport between both parties. In other words, we need to develop their trust.

For many professionals who have tried desperately to shut down a client interview which has already gone on too long and rambled into what seems like several life histories, the suggestion that we need to take more time is anathema. I am not suggesting that we need to take more time. What I am suggesting is, if we spend the time up front, we will save a lot of time later on. If we have developed a mutual understanding with clients, they will be more likely to leave us alone to get on with what they have instructed us to do!

At the most basic level, it is important to think about our body language when we first meet a client. Eye contact is important. Too many professionals have a habit of taking notes when clients start to explain what they want, which results in clients revealing their problems to the top of our heads. No wonder we are criticised for being distant and stand-offish! I have had this debate on a number of occasions with professionals, who continue to insist that taking accurate notes is more important. We usually agree that a compromise would be to keep eye contact going for the first few minutes and then explain to the client that from now on, we will have to take some notes!

Remembering the reasons why clients select their professionals, it is important to reassure the client that we have experience of this type of situation before and that we understand the client and his/her needs. We should then be able to take direct control of the meeting and focus on the required information rather than get involved in a whole lot of irrelevant and time-consuming background.

5.6.2 Reaching a basis of agreement

If we explain the options, timescales and costs to clients at the outset, we have established a basis of agreement to proceed. Most firms will want to formalise this agreement in writing. The style and length of that formalisation is up to individual firms to decide. There are a number of pro formas available, but, if they are lengthy and onerous, a covering letter explaining the key points should also be used. We do need to explore one area of this in more detail.

5.6.2.1 Let's talk about money!

We have already debated in earlier chapters the reasons why professionals find it difficult to talk about money and the problems that that causes within firms. This lack of willingness to talk about money can also cause difficulties with our relationships with clients.

Given the public perception that professionals "like to charge", many people would be astounded at the idea that professionals find it difficult to talk to clients about money. Yet, this is often the case. When we also consider that many clients instruct us without any perception of the likely cost of a piece of work, we are expecting them to write us what is effectively a blank cheque!

Professionals offer a range of explanations of why talking about money can be difficult. These include:

- *we're professionals – we don't mention money – it devalues the professional– client relationship which should be based on trust and integrity rather than hard cash;*
- *we will chase the client away if we mention costs too early;*
- *it is difficult to quote an accurate fee up front when we don't know at that stage how long the matter will take or what might be involved;*
- *I am uncomfortable about the hourly rates that we charge. I am not sure that we are worth them, don't know what they are based on and cannot justify them.*

However, this issue must be tackled, otherwise problems will appear.

The practical and professional difficulties caused by not talking about money can be considerable and risk damaging the client relationship. First of all, clients worry about costs and what our final bills are likely to be. If both parties are unclear about what has been agreed, the client is unlikely to be satisfied with what is achieved! Our time will then be taken up resolving that client's dissatisfaction and even his or her formal complaint. To resolve the issue we may need to reduce the overall fee charged. We will certainly have to wait for settlement of the fee.

The damage caused by a poor client relationship extends beyond the individual file or matter. It can harm the firm's reputation as a dissatisfied client is much more likely to tell other people about his/her views than a satisfied one!

The other problem caused by not talking about money upfront is that it becomes increasingly difficult to do so as the file progresses. As we get to know the clients better, it seems to become even more difficult to mention costs. In addition, we feel that we should hold off sending out a fee until we have something to show for it – some achievement or success for the client. This often means that months can go by with time charges and even outlays racking up without any accounting to the client. Even when we do send out a fee, we often discount it which further devalues the amount recovered.

We need to talk to clients *at the outset* about the likely timescales and costs. This helps to establish an understanding of the relationship on both sides. Clients are retaining us for our expertise provided at a commercial rate. Clients should be able to make an economic decision about whether to proceed or not, and if they go ahead, are clear about what they need to budget for.

Ways of talking about money were developed in Chapter 4. Once the firm has analysed its basis of charging and financial aspects are routinely discussed, people within the firm will become more comfortable about talking about costs with clients. Whenever possible, we should move away from any justification of our hourly rates and focus on the cost to the client if he/she does not pursue this course of action and/or the benefits that will result.

In addition, with a better awareness of the overall charges for individual files, people will be better able to give a fee quote upfront. Firms will know the likely costs and timescales of doing a piece of work, simply by monitoring files and work in progress. In addition, office systems should be designed to allow professionals to be aware of individual client work in progress and outlays as a matter of routine on a monthly basis. Interim fees should be charged wherever possible, and outlays recovered as soon as possible. All of this helps professionals to learn the likely costs and timescales for pieces of work.

For example, most solicitors know the average length of time it takes to complete a divorce and the likely costs. It is possible to give clients some indication of these, within expected parameters. Clients, on the other hand, have no feel for either of these. They will have heard stories about 5 years and bills of £20,000, but have no idea whether these are typical or even true. This is a better approach to adopt than discussing hourly rates. Providing an estimate of the total cost allows the clients to relate this to the overall outcome rather than to the hours that will be put into it. It is surely better to say "we expect the total cost will be in the region of £2,000 to £3,500" rather than "we charge out at £120 per hour and, at this stage, I have no idea about how much work is involved"!

5.7 Working with "difficult" people

We have considered the importance of developing a relationship with our clients. With some people, this can be quite difficult. There are some clients we seem to naturally get on well with. We seem to be in tune with them and what they want. This is a reflection of some of the reasons given above for why clients choose their professionals, such as empathy. Yet, there are others we seem destined never to hit it off with. However, most of us do not have the luxury to only work with people that we like. We do need to be able to develop effective communications with a wide range of people.

There are a number of techniques which can help do this. A lot of attention has been given recently to Neuro Linguistic Programming (NLP). This is a huge subject area and, if the firm finds such an approach useful, there are a number of accredited training and development programmes available (see an introduction to it in Adler, 1994). At its most simplistic level, NLP argues that people process information in a number of ways. Whilst we use all of our senses to communicate with each other, most of us have a preference for one sense over the others, and relate strongly to that sense.

For example, some people are described as auditory (hear sounds), some people are visual (see pictures) and others are kinaesthetic (touch and feel). It can help, therefore, to settle clients quickly if we can learn to communicate in the way that each prefers. In most cases, we will be talking with the client either face-to-face or on the telephone. It is possible to use key phrases to match people's preferred styles. Visual people could be asked, "What does that look like to you?" Auditory people would relate to "Does that sound like a good idea" and kinaesthetic people to "How do you feel about that?"

For example, I had a client who had the (what I perceived as irritating) habit of popping into to see me for 5 minutes without any warning. I could not under-stand why he did this rather than phone me. Yet, having a few minutes face to face with him achieved more than several phone calls. He was very visual, whilst I am auditory. He even tried to give me clues by saying "It's good to see you – you are looking well!"

Another area requires comment. We all know the importance of body language and eye contact in any relationship. We know when people are not being open by the way that they "avoid our eyes". If we care about something, we want to look people in the eyes when we talk about it. We have already commented on our habit of taking notes, with the result that clients often speak to the top of our heads! Even sitting behind a desk, although routine to many of us can place an apparent barrier between our clients and us. Most GPs now sit alongside their desks to avoid this problem, but many other professionals in office situations continue to sit at desks or around meeting tables.

5.8 Clients we would be better off without!

We all know the clients that we would be better off without. They take up hours of valuable time, constantly complain about whatever is suggested or done for them and generally cause us a lot of worry and grey hairs! When we first meet such a client, our instincts tell us that we will never satisfy him/her. We should learn to follow those instincts. It is always better not to act for that client from the outset. If we take him/her on, at best we will spend more time and effort on that file than it is worth to the client and us and at worst we may end up with a complaint against us. In all cases where we do not follow our initial instincts, it will cost us time and money. In fact, we would be better to *pay* the client to go away!

Increasing pressure on profitability has resulted in professionals not always following those instincts, with a number of cases ending up in litigation, with a lot of bad publicity. When discussing these examples with the professionals concerned, most admit that they knew the client would cause trouble from the start – either as a result of totally unrealistic expectations, and/or because of their previous track record with professionals, and/or their refusal to listen to advice.

5.9 Being client focused means managing our time!

Professionals suffer from constant interruptions all of the time. Clients expect us to respond to them instantly about even the most complex problems. Yet the nature of our work is becoming more complicated with endless sources of information to be checked and cross-checked. How can we be client responsive and still perform to an extremely high level of skill?

We have already considered that clients nowadays are much more demanding. With client loyalty a thing of the past, we have to work harder at keeping the clients we have. They expect to have access to us at all times. They are much less likely to accept what we say without question, which means that we have to spend longer with them, often for less return. Yet it is important to take time with clients – to establish rapport and a good working relationship.

Clients also have a bad habit of leaving things to the last moment. This is partly because, as already discussed, they do not want to come to see us at all and partly because they have no understanding of how much work is involved. Couple this with pressures on fee income, and we have a tendency to overcommit!

Yet, a lot of what we do is complicated and requires time to think, which means that we need to be able to concentrate, and not be interrupted. In addition, there are often risks associated with the advice that we give and we need to get it right. This puts us under additional pressure. Somehow we need to balance being responsive to individual clients at the same time as being responsible for the end product.

Effective time management implies that we have some control over our time. Many of us agree that we would have no problem managing our time if it were not for our clients! However, we need to establish some control over our working day. We will seldom achieve perfection but, if we know what we are *trying* to achieve, some of the time we will.

First of all, we need to accept that we are human beings, which implies that we will make mistakes. This is not what our professional indemnity insurers want to hear, but, even with the best people supported by the best systems, mistakes will occur. In addition, because professionals need to use their judgement in any client situation, there will always be a number of opinions as to what the best solution will be. As a result, there is no right answer. No professional likes to make mistakes. We try not to get it wrong – to protect our clients' best interests and our sanity! There are periods of time, therefore, when it is important to think and deal with difficult issues without interruptions. We can cope better with interruptions when we are doing more routine work. This means that we have to plan our work.

5.9.1 Plan our work and know ourselves!

Some people are better at managing time and themselves than others. Generally speaking, there are two distinct types of people – those who are aware of time and those who are not. People who are not aware of time do not mind being late for meetings. Those who are – hate it! Those people who have no awareness of time need to accept that they need help with their time management. They need to work with someone who is good at planning and allow that person to organise them. For those of us who are aware of time and not managing it well, this is because we are overcommitting ourselves. We need training in assertiveness and learning to say "No"!

Whatever type of person we are, we need to make an attempt to work to some form of structure. First of all, we need to look at a normal working day, week and month and mark in the time that we have no control over, where commitments must be accommodated. Routine client or project meetings need to be marked in. It is also important to put in any preparation or follow-up time that is involved. People often forget to do this, with the result that they often over-commit! It is important to include normal management tasks, such as feeing and/or file checks, and not leave them to be fitted around "more important" client work!

Then we need to look at a typical day. We need to know when we are most productive. Some of us are "larks", others "owls". Some people are therefore at their best in the mornings, others later in the day. We need to notice when we are at our best and *selfishly hoard that time*, which should be wasted on routine tasks. We should block off 1 to 2 hours every day to do difficult work or work that requires concentration, and then batch the remainder of our work around that core time. For example, if we are "larks" we should arrange meetings, site/client visits in the afternoon. This allows us part of the morning for routine work, telephone calls and correspondence and part for our core time.

Clients have to be "managed" and offered a time slot that suits them and us. If we tell them that we are most easy to reach between 3 and 5 p.m., they will start to phone us then. Remember that to do a quality job for all of our clients means that we have to stay on top of all of our workload and priorities.

In addition, it is essential to tell reception and support staff what we are trying to achieve. They will help us to manage our time and manage the clients.

We need to be careful of any tendency to overcommit. Many of us like the adrenaline rush that comes from working under pressure! Rather than assume that clients want it tomorrow, it is better to ask them the *latest* that they *need* the information. Most clients retain us for our professional judgement, not just our speed of response. We have already discussed the importance of delegating and of introducing clients to alternative people within the firm whom we trust to deal with them.

5.9.2 Be proactive!

Being proactive with clients helps to develop the client relationship as well as manage our time more effectively. Setting up routine file checks and reports will draw attention to when the file has gone quiet, rather than wait until the client complains about the lack of progress. Taking the initiative and phoning the client before he/she phones us allows us to plan when to do it rather than being interrupted, whilst doing something else. Being proactive often means doing simple things!

For example, I had a major property-investment client whose team of surveyors had to produce monthly status reports. They would all phone me over the last couple of days of each month to check the position on their individual files, with the result that I got little work done. Fed up with having my whole filing cabinet out on the floor, I instigated my own monthly report, which I sent out to their department just before the month end. The client was impressed, the surveyors were delighted and I could get on with more useful work!

5.10 Dealing with complaints

Most professional bodies have a formal process to deal with client/patient complaints. Some take a client-focused response, favouring mediation to resolve the problem. Others take a more adversarial approach. It is not always possible to avoid a client making such a complaint, but the resulting cost to the firm and the individual involved in time and worry is always significant.

Good professionals are di*stressed* when a complaint is made against them. Even when there is no merit in it, we tend to feel that we should have handled the situation better. All organisations should ensure that the individual affected should be offered whatever support is needed. That professional will feel "exposed". His or her judgement has been called into question, which is never easy to accept. Over and above that, the firm should have a process for handling client problems. This can be detailed in terms of engagement letters and/or in background information about the firm. In most firms, the senior partner shoulders the responsibility of dealing with complaints.

It is important to deal with complaints, however minor, by asking clients to expand the reason for their lack of satisfaction with the firm. Again, it is often the simplest things that upset them. (Think about a new car and a tank of petrol!) This will provide valuable information about our current services and future resource requirements. It is quite often basic elements which irritate clients the most. For example, we seldom phone into our own firms. We may be unaware that, at times, telephones are slow to be answered. Alternatively, they may be swiftly answered and then the client is left on hold as reception tries to find the person concerned! Introducing voice mail also causes frustration if people appear to be constantly unavailable.

Often, when clients appear to be unreasonable in their demands, this reflects a lack of establishing achievable expectations at the outset. It is often not a coincidence that some professionals seem to have more complaints than others. The firm should therefore develop a process for not only dealing with the individual complaint but also any adjustment required to *prevent* the problem reoccurring. There may be a system problem but, more often than not, the problems will stem from the relationship between the client and the professional.

5.11 Selling ourselves and our firm!

The importance of establishing good working relations with clients to ensure that both the client and the firm benefits from the relationship has already been discussed. We will now move onto the vexed area of "selling" which so many professionals regard as anathema to their values.

Research indicates that most new business for professional service firms comes not through direct marketing but through word-of-mouth referrals. Referrals can come from a number of sources including existing clients, friends and business connections. This provides an important reinforcement of the value of being client focused. Traditional marketing techniques are difficult to apply where we have no tangible product to show potential buyers what they will get for their money. Promotional advertising can have a place to play in our overall strategy for the firm, but it should be integrated with the style of support that clients are offered. There is little point in promoting our firm as being client focused and responsive to their needs, if a new client is passed from pillar to post when he or she first phones in!

"Selling" should be easy for professionals as we "enjoy" direct contact with our clients, with clients coming to us for help and advice. Most other sectors would be thrilled to have that level of customer contact. Where we need to improve is in *how we sell ourselves*. Too often we concentrate on the particular job in hand, focusing on the technical issue or project.

We need to take more time to provide clients with information on us and what we do. As discussed before, we must not assume that clients know what services we provide. Most of the selling of our business is carried out on our behalf by existing clients. To maximise the potential of this, they need as much information as possible about the firm to do this effectively. It is also important to include other professionals, business contacts and networks in this. This is where brochures and websites can provide a lot of core data which people can easily access.

It is also important not only to focus on "telling". We also need to develop our selling skills. Asking open questions is important – to find out about the client and his/her interests. People like to hear stories and, if provided with a story about the firm, will remember it and tell other people. Make sure, however, that the story reflects the strengths of the organisation!

People choose people! Clients will naturally select professionals who they feel comfortable with and trust. This reflects the importance of values as we tend to be more comfortable with people who share our values. It is important to always expand the number of people within the firm that the client has an opportunity to meet, which increases the chance of developing a strong relationship. Similarly, it is important to maximise the number of people we know in our client organisations. This prevents the firm from being vulnerable when the key contact moves on.

Our client analysis will have highlighted for us which clients are profitable, and where they come from. The firm should therefore be aware of its target markets. The competitor analysis will have illustrated ways where the firm can promote itself in a different way from its competitors. We need to be cautious of selling on price alone. Not only have we established that many clients pay limited attention to that aspect of selecting us and our firm, it allows clients to shop around! It is much more important to develop and emphasise the personal relationship and the understanding that we have of their situation.

Profile raising is also important to promote not only this expertise but also the values of the firm. Sponsorship is a useful mechanism to show these values in a tangible way. For example, organisations that sponsor sporting activities will not only reach their target client base but also reflect their support of team-working. Sponsoring the more "creative" arts can illustrate creativeness and innovation!

In selling terms, there is no such thing as "cold calling". On the premiss that people buy people, we should target potential new clients through our existing clients and connections. We should already know what clients or client sectors we are targeting; we should get to know as much as we can about them and, on all occasions, obtain a personal introduction to them through our existing connections. This will reassure the potential client about our professionalism and give him/her an indication of how we are likely to handle his or her work.

In summary, we need to be focused about selling. There are a number of ways of targeting activities at existing clients, at potential new clients and at business contacts in general (see Table 5.2). The ultimate aim of all of this is to create

Table 5.2 Selling tactics

New clients
- ask clients why they chose the firm? (recommended by an existing client, a contact, etc.)
- take time to tell them about the firm, what kind of work the firm as a whole handles, and what is important to *your* firm (e.g. direct partner contact)
- give them written information about the firm reinforcing what you have said
- take time to establish "rapport" (watch eye contact and body language)
- find out about the client and what is important to him/her
- really listen to the client!

Existing clients – new areas of business
- be proactive about client contact
- introduce other partners/people in the firm
- increase number of contacts in the client's organisation
- widen discussions away from the current piece of work
- having finished a piece of work try *not* to draw a line!
- carry out a review meeting or discussion and build on what you learn
- find out as much as you can about their business
- ask what they are planning to do over the next year or so
- find out as much as you can about their sector and let them know that you know
- *go and see the client!*

Referrals from contacts
- target particular contacts depending on the opportunities you want to create
- get to know them (What are their problems? How can you help them?)
- work with them on joint projects/joint proposals
- introduce them to more than one person in your firm
- again *tell* and *give* them information about the firm

Cold calling
- never cold call (always find a way of being introduced)
- do your homework (What are their problems? Who are their "key" people?)
- what other professionals do they use and why?
- tell them how you can help them – give them solutions to their problems
- again *tell* and *give* them information about the firm.

opportunities for the professional and the firm to demonstrate a high level of client satisfaction as well as develop the potential for new work.

CONCLUSIONS

This segment of the Model has concentrated on clients and our relationships with them. Power in all of the professions is moving away from the professional to the client. At the end of the day, the client is the judge of the quality of our service — not us. As a result, being client focused is essential in today's professional environment. It is equally important that we manage our time to ensure that we deliver high-quality services as cost effectively as possible. In addition, we need to achieve a balance between our professional and personal lives.

It is possible to combine all of these. First of all, we need to build relationships with our clients which they feel is responsive to their needs. We need to establish the services they expect from us and how they are delivered. We need to agree how their work will be handled and whom they can deal with when we are not available.

We need to look at our workloads and time management. We need to look at what we are doing and (with the benefit of IT) how we are doing it. We need to learn not to overcommit and take time to develop other people and systems to help us. We need to play to our strengths, know when we are most productive and jealously guard that time. We should focus on what we enjoy doing and reallocate what we do not.

Selling to clients is not any different than developing good working relationships with them. We need to provide them with information about our firm and what it does. We also need to find out what is important to them.

KEY ACTION POINTS

≫ Ask clients directly what they think of our services

≫ Maintain contact with clients even after the file is closed

≫ Expand the number of people who deal with key clients in particular

≫ Make sure databases are always up to date

≫ Establish and agree clients' expectations at the outset

≫ Develop and retain their trust

≫ Talk about fees and costs upfront

≫ Be responsive and proactive

≫ Give clients information about the firm, its services and values

➢ Communicate effectively

➢ Get rid of the clients we are better off without

➢ Don't overcommit

➢ Deal with complaints

➢ Remember people buy people!

6. Options for Development

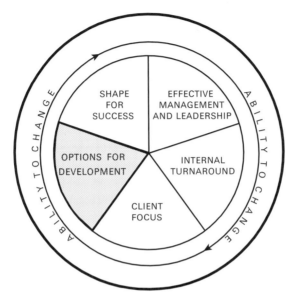

THE MODEL FOR SUCCESS

6.1 Introduction

The importance of being client focused has already been established. This requires current and up-to-date information about what our clients want and what they will want from us in the future. This segment of the Model allows us to look at the future of our organisations and, in particular, what options we have.

Most writers on business strategy make much use of the phrase "strategic management". By that, they mean that organisations need to decide their future direction and find the resources to get them there. Thompson's model (1997) has already been discussed (Section 2.3). It uses three overlapping circles which illustrate that, for any business to operate successfully, it has to do so where people's values, its resources and the external environment overlap. Segments 1 and 2 of the Model have provided us with a detailed understanding of the first two. These make up the framework of what is feasible and acceptable to us. We now need to analyse the market place and develop our understanding of it to allow us to select the best options for developing the firm. To do this, we need to be able to identify what future clients of the firm will want from us. This requires knowledge of market trends.

This chapter is designed to help us take control of our future. It allows us to identify these external pressures, sort and prioritise them, match them with the values and resources of our firms and develop strategies to support them.

6.2 Taking back control!

Having the right product at the right time in the right place for the right market is the basic premiss of most business success. This implies knowledge of customers and competitors. Over and above that, it implies an awareness and understanding of how the market place currently operates and how it will operate in the future (i.e. who will be its future customers and competitors). Given the resource base of most professional firms, it is unlikely that we can directly influence the market-place. It is essential therefore that we develop ways of coping with its variations.

Chapter 2 highlighted some of the challenges facing most professionals. Increasing consumerism and the impact of IT, in particular, have resulted in a feeling of being overwhelmed by pressure to adapt and change. Many people are confused about *how* to respond, unable to prioritise which of these pressures are capable of being managed and controlled. People seem generally aware that "things are not what they were". Some people feel unable to plan ahead, arguing that "there is little point as things change so fast". Some people are uneasy and want clarity. Others appear to be blindly indifferent. Most firms want to be more in control and to have some sense of what needs to be done. How can we have any long-term plan for the business when things change so fast?

As we have already discussed, planning is important, even if it only allows the firm to focus on its priorities. To help us understand the market place, we need to develop a process of analysis, which can help to:

- put issues into perspective;
- make an assessment of their impact and importance;
- identify some positive (defensive or proactive) steps to be taken;
- allow people to talk from an informed position rather than subjective bias; and
- focus decision making.

Developing strategies for the future is not an exact science. There is no one "right answer", and even when firms adopt a particular option, they will never know whether another one would have been better. All they will know is that it would have been different. Intuition will play a part in the ultimate decision, as most entrepreneurs will confirm. As we know, partnerships are based on consensus. These decisions about the future direction of the firm will require the agreement of all of the partners (and other influencers). Professionals like to analyse and debate! It is important therefore to involve as many people as possible in information gathering and debating as this helps to educate and involve everyone. We need to recognise the importance of both intuition and analysis.

6.3 Understanding the market place

Most professionals now accept the impact of the market place on their firms. They have experienced its direct effect on fee levels in particular. However, the pace of change is increasing. With the market place moving at such an apparently alarming rate, external awareness of that marketplace and its future trends is crucial. To devise a strategy for the firm and to make any kind of plans for the future requires accurate, up-to-date knowledge of the market place.

Trends are important for a number of reasons. They are vitally important in any selection of future direction. They also help to identify potential new business opportunities and establish both short- and long-term objectives. Sources of these trends are many and varied. The construction industry often leads changes and influences a wide range of professionals. Economic indicators illustrate a raft of areas where future business may be gained and lost. As shown in Chapter 2, it is possible to identify trends which directly affect all of the professions, albeit at different stages. For example, the architects and surveying professions felt the impact of information technology before law and accountancy. The legal and medical professions have been the two most strongly affected by the impact of increased indemnity claims by private individuals.

Conferences, competitors, formal and informal networks, outside interests and involvement all widen people's perspectives about what is happening as well as encouraging a sense of proportion which can often be lost in firms battling to cope with fee targets. Again, research (Gibb, 1984; Turok, 1988; MacMillan, et al., 1989) reinforces the value of bringing in external advisers as many of the firms that do so perform better than those that do not.

Taking time out to look longer term is important. Many of the most successful businesses adopt this as a matter of routine. They encourage senior managers to take sabbaticals, partly to allow them to re-energise, but also to let them "go fishing"! Some of the best examples of accelerated growth have come from anticipating future client demands; for example, software companies which developed call-centre support systems before that market took off.

6.4 Strategic thinking

Thinking strategically requires two elements – structured analysis and lateral thinking. This reflects the two sides of our brain – the "left" or analytical side and the "right" or creative side. A lot of research has been done in this area, with De Bono one of the main writers on the theme of creative thinking (De Bono, 1992). Most people are good at one or the other, with some generalisations being made about individual professions!

Architects tend to be "right" brained, engineers and surveyors "left"! This implies that strategic thinking is best achieved through a combination of inputs from a range of individuals.

Everyone should be encouraged to be more externally aware. Reading widely is important. Publications, such as *The New Scientist*, can be an excellent source of future trends and developments. There is always a risk that we become so focused on the narrow areas in which we work that we miss something which could have a significant impact on us and the way that we work. Everyone knows the story of lobsters not noticing that the water in the cooking pot is getting hotter!

First (Stage 1), people who enjoy analysis and structure should be made responsible for watching for trends in the market place, including changes in clients' demands and changes in competitors. They should report on these on a routine basis to the firm as a whole.

Second (Stage 2), there will be some people in the firm who enjoy lateral and/ or conceptual thinking as a matter of course. They should be encouraged and allowed to do so. Depending on the size of the firm, a strategy group should be established or an individual given responsibility to generate ideas and report regularly on these to the whole firm. This is a different exercise than the trend analysis, and requires "out-of-the box" thinking. Many of the partners who are the most difficult to manage are often the people best suited to generate these conceptual responses! This is one way that they can be brought into the team and help them to understand the importance of a concerted response.

Third (Stage 3), the firm as a whole should consider these trends and debate these ideas – talk them through, agree or disagree and select some options. As indicated above, it is important to involve everyone. This helps to educate people about the reasons why change may be needed, the options for change and again, based on factual data and analysis, it provides the framework for rational debate. It also allows the firm to identify options in good time to be able to respond to them – to find the resources, the skills and expertise to carry them through.

These stages illustrate a process, close to that developed by Johnson and Scholes (1997) and Stacey (1993) who describes it as "discover, choose, act". In summary, developing strategies for the future of the firm includes the following steps:

- analyse the market place to identify significant trends;
- develop some choices – think creatively;
- check these choices against your values;
- then check them against your resources (current and future);
- choose an option;
- select the best way of achieving it;
- start to implement it; and
- review progress, check for external changes and adjust.

Always remember that strategy is untidy! It is never as clear-cut as people may think. Yes, it is important to be aware of and respond to the market, but too much change unsettles people. It is important therefore to take control and be proactive, rather than reactive. Section 6.5 looks at each stage of the process and develops some tools to help do it.

6.5 Stage 1 What is the market place telling us?

First of all, the external environment should be analysed. This begins the process of allowing us to take control, by providing a structure to interpret which market pressures affect us directly. We need to start by scanning the market, which can include the commissioning of clippings services, sector reports, and business and market research information. The problem nowadays is not getting access to the information but rather how to narrow it down to what is relevant! We will already have a good idea of what sectors are important to us and where our best clients come from. These sectors, in particular, must be scanned to ensure that there are no future developments which are likely to have a direct impact on the firm. Reports should therefore be prepared on these key-client sectors, preferably by in-house personnel. This allows the firm to learn from and adapt the data gathered. Whilst using external services for this exercise may appear quicker, it often leads to reports which lie unread. It is the application of the information (rather than the information itself) which is important. We need to interpret the data and respond to what we learn from it.

In addition to these sector reports, we also need to scan the wider market place. This happens as a matter of accident as we all keep abreast of television, radio and news programmes, read newspapers and magazines and talk in general with people. All of this information is useful and provides the basis for a more general analysis of future trends. There are some specific publications on "futures". *Time Magazine* continues to be one of the most succinct précis of global events and it is well worth leaving where people can quickly scan through it (reception areas and kitchens!). Another interesting source are publications of the Royal Society of Arts (1998; 1999). The Department of Trade and Industry (1998; 1999; 2000) has published a number of reports looking at future competitiveness which are well worth getting hold of.

Having gathered all this information, how do we structure its analysis? How do we sort and prioritise what is important to the firm and its future, so that those areas which are important form the basis of specific actions? A range of models and tools is available to structure such an exercise. For example, the EPISTLE model (Robertson, 1994, see Table 6.1) and Porter's 5 Forces (1980) allow grouping of key external influences. They help to facilitate a structured discussion, as well as identify key priorities.

It is important that this analysis results in specific responses. An action plan should be agreed based on the following questions:

- What is the trend?
- What does it mean for the firm?
- What specific action needs to be taken?
- Who will be responsible for it?
- What resources will be needed?
- How will its success be measured?
- When will progress be reviewed?

Table 6.1 Generic EPISTLE trends

Economic
- current economic performance
- influence of government policies
- influence of fiscal policies
- current interest rates
- influence of European Union
- current business performance
- increasing global influence
- increasing IT dependency
- increasing number of small businesses
- shift from manufacture to services
- skills shortages

Political
- stability of government
- increasing global interactions
- increased integration with Europe
- increasing influence of regions
- favourable climate for small-business support
- increasing emphasis on entrepreneurial skills
- erosion of monopoly position on products and services
- increasing partnership between private and public sectors
- increasingly stringent external regulations

Intellectual
- increasing importance in economy
- increasing importance in business
- increasing importance of knowledge at micro- and macro-level

Social
- gap between rich and poor increasing
- shift in work patterns
- increasing numbers of women working
- increasing familiarity with IT
- increase in direct purchase by consumers
- increasing numbers of people working from home
- work becoming location independent
- decline of job security
- increasing acceptance of self-employed status
- increasing number of car users
- increasing demand for leisure activities
- increasing numbers of divorces
- increasing numbers of single parents
- decline in numbers of school leavers
- increasing numbers in further/higher education
- increasing social diversity

(continued)

Table 6.1 (cont.)

- ageing population
- increasing consumerism

Technological
- increasing speed of technological change
- increasing dependence on IT
- increasing worldwide access to information
- increasing speed of access/business response
- improved and cheaper communications
- reducing costs of technology
- shift in skill levels
- skill shortages
- videoconferencing replacing face-to-face meetings
- possibility of 24-hour access
- impact of dot.com companies on market place

Legal
- increasing complexity of legislation
- increasing layering of influences – regional, national, European, global
- increasing consumerism

Environmental
- increasing emphasis on business context
- increasing legislation
- decline in quality of environment
- pressure on finite resources
- potential change in climate
- increasing importance of water in global context
- increase in demands for energy

I will illustrate the above using my own firm as an example. Given the current trend of downsizing and outsourcing, the number of consultants and the amount of consultancy work has increased. There is no real quality control in this sector as there is no overall professional body which regulates entry and standards. As with any professional service, it is difficult for clients to assess the expertise of people offering consultancy services. What that means for my firm is that I have to develop ways of increasing my profile and showing my expertise. Apart from continuing to do high-quality client work, and developing a website, the specific action I decided to take was to write this book. I had the resources to do it as I had direct experience of working both in and with a wide range of professionals and their organisations. I also enjoy writing. The additional resource that I needed was the time to do it! The measure of its success will be whether the book sells and whether people feel that it has helped them and their organisations. I will be able to review both of these on an ongoing basis!

6.5.1 The EPISTLE Model

We have established the need to identify both the current and future trends influencing the market place in which we operate. The EPISTLE model (Robertson, 1994) allows the identification of key trends which need to be managed, sorting them into seven headings:

- economic trends, such as general trading conditions – within the UK and the world;
- political influences, such as the current emphasis on generating business start-ups and more "entrepreneurial activity";
- intellectual issues which will affect the firm in particular, such as the increasing importance of protecting intellectual property given the impact of the Internet;
- social trends, such as increasing numbers of women working and the effect that will have on the demand for childcare and/or convenience foods;
- technological advances which will affect the way that we and our clients do business, such as improved and cheaper communications;
- legal issues that will influence the market place, such as competition law; and
- environmental aspects which more and more organisations and individuals now have to take into consideration.

Table 6.1 shows some of these trends (relevant at the time of writing!).

It is important for organisations to examine these trends in detail and check whether they are valid for their particular situation. They should spend some time generating a list of their own under each of the seven headings. Not every trend will have a direct effect on every organisation. Some will be more significant than others. Some may be neutral. In each case, we need to decide whether it poses a threat or an opportunity?

For example, for firms specialising in the design of large headquarters, they may see the increase in the number of self-employed as a threat. For firms specialising in small-business accountancy services, the same trend will be seen as an opportunity. If it poses a threat for our design firm, what can we do about it? We may be able to target clients who still want large headquarters in the short term, but if trends indicate that work is becoming location irrelevant, this would indicate that the demand for large headquarters will continue to drop. If the trend poses an opportunity, how can we respond to it? How can we position the firm to maximise its potential? For example, some accountancy firms have maximised the potential of more small-business owners by helping them come to grips with increasing regulatory requirements through the development of simple-to-use software.

Some trends may not be in our direct control. If not, what are we able to influence and how? For example, we may decide that the current IT skill shortages will directly limit our ability to develop new services. How can we influence the supply of suitably qualified graduates? As a result, some forward-looking software companies are "growing their own" by working in close partnerships with universities.

This illustrates the importance of integrating significant trends. By combining the impact of one with the influence of another, it is possible to build up a series of related responses. There is little point in developing actions which contradict each other and waste limited resources and energy!

6.5.2 Porter's 5 Forces (adapted)

Porter's 5 Forces model (1980) encourages organisations to prioritise the market-place pressures acting on it by grouping a number of external factors in order of importance. As with the EPISTLE model, it is designed to help organisations manage these influences by sorting them into priorities and responses. I have adapted Porter's approach to better suit professionals and their organisations and as a result, have generated six rather than five headings. We need to consider how vulnerable we are to the following factors:

1. the power and influence of our clients;
2. our supply of quality staff;
3. our suppliers;
4. the threat of other firms to entering into and exiting from the market;
5. the threat of competitors; and
6. the threat of substitute services.

Sections 6.5.2.1–6.5.2.6 explore these headings in the context of the typical professional firm. Again, the actions suggested are generic and should not be assumed as directly relevant. We need to carry through this exercise in the context of our own organisation and situation.

6.5.2.1 The power and influence of our clients

As with all businesses, professional firms are dependent on clients. In recent years, clients have become much more price sensitive in their purchase of professional services. The abolition of scale fees has encouraged clients to shop around. However, as clients find it difficult to appreciate the technical expertise of what we do, they find it difficult to compare firms and what each offers. At least, when we compare the price of holidays, we can establish whether we are being offered a four- or five-star hotel. Firms need to be aware of this price sensitivity as well as explaining what will be included in the service provided.

Historically, it was not easy to change professional service providers. Key information and data was held by them, and clients who moved around too much were considered "risky". As a result, clients stayed with firms often for generations and even commercial clients would boast that they had been with the same firm for many years. However, as change became more accepted, as families no longer stayed with the same firms without question and as commercial clients themselves became more "changeable", client loyalty became a thing of the past. Clients became and continue to be much more willing and able to move around.

The power and influence of clients is therefore potentially high. Key actions could include:

- being accessible to clients and delivering value for money;
- maintaining client contact as much as possible;
- tailoring services to meet clients' needs; and
- developing ways of increasing clients' "ties" to the firm.

6.5.2.2 Our supply of quality staff

Any service business is heavily dependent on its staff to deliver a high-quality, consistent and cohesive service. The most common complaint of most successful firms is the difficulty that they have in attracting and keeping high-quality people. Firms need to develop strategies to address this, such as looking at recruitment, career structures and the use of external qualifications for non-professional staff. All of these should include succession planning, secondment options and client project work.

Our vulnerability to the supply of quality staff is therefore potentially high. Key actions could include:

- developing strong recruitment and induction practices;
- introducing regular review meetings on a one-to-one basis to identify future training and support;
- offering clear career paths and development opportunities, such as mentoring and secondment; and
- developing reward mechanisms.

6.5.2.3 Our suppliers

The bargaining power of all our suppliers should be considered to ascertain whether we have a particular vulnerability in any area.

In particular, with the increasing importance of and dependence on technology, the organisation's dependency on these suppliers should be addressed. Firms should not make themselves vulnerable, either financially or operationally. If the integration of technology is an important element in the strategic growth of the firm, the firm should ensure that it has in-house expertise in that area, not just enthusiastic amateurs or staff trained in small elements. It should invest in both the resources and skills necessary. Not only will that reduce its dependence on its suppliers, it will also allow the firm to develop its own systems to maximise its strategy.

Our vulnerability to technology suppliers in particular is on the increase. Key actions could include:

- developing in-house expertise in technology;
- ensuring staff are well trained in their use of technology; and
- maintaining close links with hardware and software suppliers.

6.5.2.4 The threat of other firms entering into and exiting from the market

This factor requires consideration of the ease with which other businesses can move in and set up in the market place. For example, the high cost of setting up and equipping a highly technical production line means that the difficulty of entry into the manufacture of high-specification valve products is high. However, for a professional firm, particularly as the cost of technology support comes down, the cost of setting up in business is low. Couple this with the general dissatisfaction that many professionals feel within existing partnerships means that the number of new small professional businesses being established is on the increase.

Exit from a professional practice is not easy. It is difficult to wind up a professional firm, as many client obligations continue after the end of the particular piece of work. Professional indemnity often requires professionals to maintain cover in force even after they cease to be involved in the firm. This results in firms continuing on, even when they are inherently unviable, because of the difficulties of shutting them down.

With ease of entry into the market high and the difficulty of exit from the market also high, this results in the market place "backing up" – with new firms coming in, and older firms unable to exit.

This threat is therefore potentially high. Key actions could focus on:

- ensuring that we keep and reward our high-quality people;
- maintaining client loyalty; and
- managing the firm to ensure current profitability and future viability.

6.5.2.5 The threat of competitors

Most professionals agree that the market place has become much more competitive in recent years. Not only are we facing more direct competition, as already indicated before, we are facing increasing indirect competition. Accountants and lawyers are chasing the same type of work, architects and building surveyors are vying for property refurbishments, banks and building societies are moving into financial services. This means that clients can be attracted away via the core products of these businesses and then sold on services which traditionally were the domain of other professionals. Some of these competitors have a larger resource base and are able to provide "lost leaders" to attract clients to them in the first instance.

This tactic is also used by our direct competitors, with firms undercutting each other in an attempt to capture new clients.

The threat of competitors is therefore potentially high. Key actions to address both direct and indirect competition could include:

- maintaining client awareness and relationships;
- ensuring that fees are cost effective to both the firm and its clients; and
- developing joint ventures with other professionals to allow the firm to service and support all of its clients' needs.

6.5.2.6 The threat of substitute services

On first consideration, the threat of substitute services seems remote. How can clients find substitutes for high-quality professional expertise and experience? However, when consideration is given to the development of software packages which allow tax returns to be completed, wills to be prepared and building designs to be drawn, this threat gains significance. Clients are now able to carry through many of the traditional professional services themselves and this trend will increase. If the firm is heavily dependent on the services which are directly affected, it is likely that profit margins will first of all erode as the price is driven down and then demand will disappear completely.

Some firms have responded by altering the services they provide. Accountants, rather than block clients doing more themselves, now work with clients by providing them with the software to do it. They can then concentrate on the more lucrative (and interesting) work.

The bargaining power of substitute services is potentially increasing. Key actions could include:

- careful monitoring of software and on-line developments against the services provided by the firm;
- adjusting the firm's service delivery to match what clients will do for themselves; and
- making adjustments to our range of services to close any gaps that the loss of that work will create.

6.5.2.7 In summary

The above analysis illustrates how the Model can help analyse these pressure points. As it is based on a generic firm, all six elements seem to indicate high priorities. It is important not to panic and make assumptions that this will be the case for all of us! Completing this exercise for our own organisations will allow us to identify where we are less vulnerable than other firms and/or sectors. Some elements may be working to our advantage, others may be neutral and others will pose significant threats.

For example, a firm, which has established a niche position in architectural design, will be well placed to defend against competitors. The threat of substitute products will be low as it is difficult to reproduce its high level of expertise. With close client connections, it should be able to manage the power and influence of its clients. Its priority will be to ensure the commitment of its expert and experienced people, who maintain these relations and high-quality work. It will be important to retain them as it may be possible that key people could leave and set up in competition, as entry into the market will be easy for them, which would then increase its competitor rivalry!

As with the first Model, it is essential to work out which have a direct impact and develop key actions to ensure that the implications are addressed.

6.5.3 *"Futures thinking"*

Another useful exercise to generate future trends is to encourage people to think much longer term, say 10 or 20 years ahead. This allows people to be really adventurous in their thinking, rather than being limited by practical problems which may occur in the short term. Interestingly, research indicates that the further people can think into the future, the more competent they are in dealing with issues today. (For more information on this, see Cooper and Sawaf, 1998, p. 249.)

Some people may argue that there is little point in trying to analyse so far ahead given that they currently have difficulty planning in the short term! However, some sense of direction of future trends can be achieved by thinking 20 years ahead. It is not possible to be accurate about this. For example, some predictions for the year 2000 were wrong. It was predicted in 1967, that by the year 2000, viral diseases would be almost eliminated, planets would be colonised and nuclear power would be a major energy source. Correct predictions from 1967 included the development of artificial intelligence and a global library and that genetic chemistry would correct hereditary defects (World Future Society, 1999). Publications and associations, such as *The Futurist* and the World Future Society, provide excellent summaries of such trends.

Again, it is important to identify key trends and apply them to our particular situations. For example, given the impact on our physical environment of virtual-design options, will we still have the same demand to move home every few years or will we simply adjust the options we currently have? If we will soon be able to live healthy and fit into our nineties, how will this affect our attitude towards work and retirement? What will be the impact on the relationships that we develop with people? What will be the impact on our demand for professional services?

Another technique was developed by Royal Dutch Shell in the late 1960s and early 1970s, allowing it to manage some of the variations in oil demand during the 1970s and 1980s (Wack, 1985). "Scenario planning" involves the consideration of a number of scenarios based on an analysis of current and future trends, and their implications. Whilst most professional firms do not have the resource base and/or expertise to develop these scenarios in detail, it is still possible to develop a number of "scenarios" of the future. What would be the best case scenario for our firm? What would it look like? What would people be saying about us? What would it feel like to be a member of the firm? How would we achieve this? What steps would have to be taken to get us there?

Similarly, it is a good idea to involve the doubting Thomases of the organisation, and ask them to develop the worst case scenario. Then ask them to identify ways of stopping that happening! In addition, if at all possible, organisations should widen the pool of people involved in the process to include outsiders, clients and other sectors.

6.5.4 *Caveat – do the analysis and ACT on it!*

Firms need to be careful about the length of time that this exercise can take. Professionals are good at thinking analytically and can be guilty of indulging themselves in this type of exercise forever, constantly seeking more and more information. Given the wealth of material that exists, there is a danger that the process of analysis goes on and on! Remember that other people in the market place are doing the same and that if we analyse an issue to death, we may miss the opportunities that this exercise may present.

6.6 Stage 2 What choices do we have?

We now need to put the opportunities created by the above exercise into practice. We may have identified a significant trend which we need to capitalise on, such as the growth in leisure activities. There are a range of options open to most organisations. At the most simple level, these include:

- getting bigger or smaller;
- expanding upwards or sideways,
- staying in the existing market;
- moving into a new market; or
- giving up all together!

Assuming that the firm wants to stay in business, we need to start generating some choices and see how suitable they would be. Within the current market place, most professional firms are under pressure at the moment to improve profit levels. Some may be happy to maintain current fee levels but reduce operational costs, others may be anxious to increase fee income and reduce overheads, others may already be tightly managed but want to accelerate their income growth. There are a number of ways to achieve these aims but, first of all, we need to decide which is our priority. Are we happy with the firm the size it is, but want to increase our profitability? Or do we want to grow? If the first option is selected then the firm will need to concentrate on improving internal efficiency. If the second option is chosen then there are a number of ways of achieving it.

Ansoff's framework (1968) illustrates the basic options available. Firms can opt to:

- increase fee levels by selling more of the same services to existing clients;
- increase fee levels by selling new services to existing clients;
- increase fee levels by selling the same services to new clients; or
- increase fee levels by selling new services to new clients.

Whatever option is selected, there are a number of ways to support it which will be developed in more detail later in this chapter. For example, some of the major accountancy firms have been working backwards up their "supply chain" by building solicitors into their service delivery. Some have achieved this through directly employing lawyers, others by entering into alliances with law firms.

Porter (1985) offers generic strategies based on cost and/or differentiation. Firms can position themselves as cost leaders in the market, or can differentiate themselves from their competitors. Some professional firms have successfully adopted a competitive strategy based on lowest costs, both internally and externally. This has validity as long as it is consciously adopted and not merely the result of external pressures to reduce the level of fees charged. Given the personal nature of professional services and given the reasons identified before as to why clients choose professionals, a strategy based on differentiation makes commercial sense. A niche strategy can work well as it allows the firm to position itself in the market, focusing its attention on a specific sector. This suits the limited resource base of smaller organisations, as well as allowing the firm to target its profile- and image-raising activities. However, the choice is up to the organisation to make.

6.6.1 Think creatively!

The essential element here is to think creatively! Many professionals have been trained to think analytically and objectively to elicit the facts and apply them to principles or precedents, to narrow the focus of client discussions and ask closed questions to limit discussions and options. This is the firm's opportunity to think differently from its competitors and come up with a unique answer!

Another problem here is that professionals are often limited by the rules of their professional bodies and their professional values. For example, expanding by absorbing other professionals is not yet open to everyone. For those that do, partnerships of architects and surveyors offer the option of exciting varieties of client services. They offer the potential for both creative ideas and practical (right and left brain) solutions. The other factor is that most professionals want to stay professional! Too often I am asked in by firms to discuss the future direction of the business, with partners assuring me that they are willing to consider any options to allow the firm to recover/respond to market pressures. Inevitably these options become constrained to what that firm and its partners are comfortable with.

Successful creative solutions have been found. There are a number of firms who have changed their core services or adapted the emphasis they place on the professional element of their service. For example, Scottish law firms now work with English law matters and vice versa. Surveyors have moved from technical work to consultancy work. Architects have reduced their involvement in production and increased their emphasis on design. As a result, some firms are extremely successful *in the same market place* as firms that are "dying".

As a starting point, the results of the analysis of the market place should be presented to the firm. This ensures that people are aware of the issues within the market place and where the main opportunities lie. The strategy group or lateral thinkers should be asked to generate as many ideas as possible to tackle these issues and develop some options. They should be encouraged to think as if they had a "magic wand", rather than make any judgement at this stage, about whether the idea was sensible or practical. It is important not to limit what they think are options for the firm without offering them for discussion first. This will generate more possibilities and energise everyone to get involved. In addition, taking the time out to think about this is vital – trying to fit this around client meetings and workloads is impossible. People need to be taken out of the office environment as otherwise the day-to-day pressures limit their ability to think wider and longer term.

6.6.2 Making our choice

The result of this exercise should then be presented to all of the partners for discussion. The firm needs to decide which of these options is most suited to it. This requires a check against those that match its values and its resources. Its values are not likely to change in the future, and provide a constant frame of reference. To a certain extent, current resources will influence what is possible, but the organisation may select an option which involves expanding the resources considerably. That will then become an important element in the route that the firm takes to get there.

For example, if a firm decides that it wants to expand its range of client services, it can do so by:

- developing the range of expertise of its current people;
- headhunting key people;
- retaining expert consultants;
- amalgamating with another firm; or
- developing a joint venture.

6.6.3 What fits with our values?

The first check that has to be undertaken is do(es) the option(s) fit with the agreed values of the firm. This reinforces the importance of the Model – that we need to start with managing people through their values. There is little point in generating a range of options which clash with the values of the firm.

For example, the firm may decide that to respond to market pressures, it needs to concentrate on certain core elements of client services. This will result in a different blend of skills than currently available. It therefore has two main options – to get rid of people without these skills and recruit new people or it can retrain those who have the ability and willingness to do so. If the firm's values stress the importance of supporting people, the second option is the only one that is acceptable to it.

Checking against the firm's values is the first point of reference when deciding between options. The second point of reference is whether the option is practical.

6.6.4 What is practical?

This creative thinking, however, does need to be balanced with practicality, which is why the exercises described above are worthwhile. By carrying through an EPISTLE and/or Porter's exercise the firm has analysed its pressures and priorities. Generating creative solutions ensures that these are put into that context and addressed.

The "practicality" check requires firms to act within the requirement of their professional rules and regulations. It also requires consideration of the resources to carry it through. For example, if the firm is considering rapid expansion, most professional partnerships cannot sell equity in the firm to outsiders (i.e. non-professionals) in the same way that limited companies can bring in venture capital. Partnerships are therefore forced to consider short-term borrowing or asking the partners to put in more capital. This inevitably impacts on the decision to adopt any long-term strategy where the resultant beneficiaries of such an approach may be the younger and indeed successive partners.

Practicality also requires a close look at the people skills available. Many a partnership decision has seemed like a good idea at the time, but when it comes to implementation the firm lacks the technical ability to do it. For example, if the firm decides to become a leader in client-tailored solutions, does it have the level of expertise to deliver them without buying in expensive and hard-to-retain expertise? Strategies can be all very well in theory but difficult to apply in practice. Again, if the firm decides to cope with change by investing heavily in technology, are the people in the firm able and willing to learn new computer skills?

6.7 Stage 3 How are we going to get there?

Having worked through the analysis exercise(s) to identify the potential that exists in the market place and the threats that need to be addressed, having generated some options to respond to them, tempered them with the values of the firm and identified which are practical within the current and future resources, and made its choice, the firm needs now to look at what practical strategies exist to help it achieve what it wants.

There are a number of ways of implementing any major strategy or change of emphasis for the firm. Common options include natural growth (which provides the advantage of stability and the disadvantage of slowness), or one of the more adventurous and faster options of amalgamations or joint ventures.

6.7.1 Natural growth

Natural growth implies the steady and incremental development of the firm, building on its inherent strengths and addressing its weaknesses. Some firms have been very successful with this approach and have more than maintained their position. We can all think of examples of firms who have steadily increased their market position, without a great deal of fuss or speculation. The strategic disadvantages associated with this approach are that it tends to be slow and can lull people into a lack of external awareness and general complacence.

In the past, most firms made the decision to grow organically. This allowed the steady flow of young professionals through training to partnership, and then up the letterhead to senior partner and retiral. This was the traditional approach, with many of us now in our forties and fifties happy to support such an option and structure. However, this option is becoming increasingly limited.

There are two main reasons for this. The first is that this response is too slow for many current market pressures. Many firms are being forced to invest heavily in technology, putting pressure on capital and ways of working. Smaller firms may find it difficult to fund such investment. Increasing complexity is putting pressure on professionals at an early stage to become more specialised, which again encourages firms to become bigger and/or more selective in the clients they serve.

The other reason is that younger professionals are simply more mobile. They are less likely to be enticed by the carrot of partnership than their previous generation. They observe the behaviour of the partners with interest. They are certainly aware of the financial pressures on the firm and, with unlimited liability, they often question the risk-and-reward equation. The other side of the coin is that, even in larger partnerships, it is increasingly difficult to offer everyone an equity place. In addition, it is much more professionally acceptable to move between firms. In the past, if a young professional moved around too much, he or she may have been regarded as at best "unstable" or even professionally "questionable". All of this means that it is difficult for firms to retain quality people because good professionals can always find positions elsewhere. Because of this, existing partners are unwilling to delegate their client work to younger members of the team, fearing that they will leave and take the clients with them. This produces severe problems of manageability with senior people doing work which they should leave to others and young professionals unhappy about not getting the chance to do quality work and improve their skills!

The key to growing naturally is the organisation's ability to retain high-quality people. We have already considered the importance of values to professionals and their behaviour. It is therefore important to involve young professionals in these types of discussions at as early a stage as possible, talk to them regularly on a one-to-one basis, recognise their contribution and give them the opportunity to learn. As developed in Section 3.4, they are unlikely to be solely motivated by financial reward, but will respond to being given responsibility, challenging and quality client work, supported by role models and/or mentors. This is true of all high-quality people, whether trained as professionals or not.

It is also important to challenge any assumptions that are made about the future shape and skill base of the firm. The analysis exercise will have shown certain future trends that are likely to have an impact on the demand for and type of client services, which need to be built into any organic growth plans. For example, does the firm have sufficient environmental expertise? Will it need to develop a more multidiscipline shape?

Organic growth takes time. If the organisation decides to adopt a faster route, it has a number of options available to it.

6.7.2 Accelerated growth

There are a number of ways of accelerating the growth of the firm. These include buying another firm, merging with another firm or entering into some kind of relationships with other firm(s). Each has distinct advantages and disadvantages, but whatever is chosen must bring positive benefits to the firm which could include:

- increasing the partner profile;
- increasing the profile of the firm;
- increasing the skill base and expertise;
- providing succession planning and/or an exit strategy;
- increasing the resource base;
- producing economies of scale;
- increasing the quality of the client base;
- increasing the future potential of the client base; and/or
- providing geographical or service expansion.

It is too easy to assume that some of these must happen by default. It is important to identify which will be delivered by the merger option and develop ways of measuring whether they have been achieved.

6.7.2.1 Growth by acquisitions

Some firms may identify the opportunity to develop by acquiring other firms. Like any option, this should be planned and thought through. Too often acquisitions happen almost by accident, as a result of the retirement of a sole trader, and/or an unexpected death with no succession planning in place. Whilst such situations may present an opportunity, firms need to carefully consider why they should acquire that firm. If the other firm was already in decline, they may be acquiring a distraction to their core business or, indeed, damage their own reputation.

Even the most entrepreneurial have had their fingers burnt by paying too high a price for such a purchase. The value of professional firms is difficult to assess, with a great deal of client loyalty focused on the individual professional rather than the firm as a whole. This makes it difficult to guarantee how much of the business will successfully transfer over to the new firm.

6.7.2.2 Amalgamations

Amalgamations were a very popular strategic choice in the late 1980s and early 1990s. As outlined above, these were a response to the pressure to become more specialised, and/or to expand geographically and/or to increase the resource base (especially to pay for IT investment). Having been involved myself in an ambitious one in 1987, I would caution against adopting such a choice without due consideration of the amount of commitment it requires. Quite apart from the need to manage and resolve any partner-level behaviours, staff can be extremely unsettled by a merger. It is almost impossible to underestimate the amount of time that will be spent massaging staff and partner resistance!

However, amalgamations can be a useful strategy. The key is to ensure that that the advantages outweigh the disadvantages. The combined product must be better than its individual elements to justify the considerable investment in management and resources. Again, as previously discussed, values are the driver. Both firms must have the same values and drivers – in essence the same ethos and culture.

Values are of vital importance, and assumptions about these should not be made. Both firms should look at and identify their common values. An amalgamation between a firm which values a high level of partner input into client service delivery will not match one that places a high value on having "fewer chiefs and more indians".

Identifying positive drivers is important. These can include achieving economies of scale, of succession planning or expanding the areas of expertise on offer. Where the firms are merging for defensive reasons, avoid developing negative drivers, such as cost cutting, closure of offices, and staff reduction. Whilst these may be the outcomes of some of the positive drivers (i.e. economies of scale), they can colour people's attitudes towards the amalgamation and, as a result, prejudice its likely success.

If some of the key players are against the merger, it is important to address this upfront, otherwise a great deal of time and effort can be wasted. It is much better to debate and reject an amalgamation option than take up months of meetings talking round peripheral issues.

Both firms must feel that they are contributing and gaining something. Compromise may be required but, from the outset, discussions must develop openness and trust. Common aims and objectives must be debated and agreed. Quite apart from the vexed issues of unlimited liability, people are unlikely to share clients and expertise if this commonality is not established.

In addition, both firms must see this as a long-term commitment. The payback to such a strategy is unlikely to be quick. As already outlined, many days and months of work will be involved even before the merger is agreed. Often, it will take at least 2 years before any impact on the bottom line is perceived, and in the short term will require considerable investment in time and other resources.

Once the values and drivers have been agreed, then both firms will need to look at the figures. The combined figures can be developed making certain assumptions about the future size of the combined firm. The outcome of this exercise must support the aims and objectives of the amalgamation and confirm that the joint operation will be viable. All of these elements must be in place before the amalgamation proceeds. From the outset, everyone should be clear about what we are doing, why we are doing it and what we expect to get out of it.

6.7.2.3 Joint ventures

Joint ventures are being used increasingly in the commercial environment. They allow the coming together of separate businesses to satisfy customer or client demands and provide a wider pool of resources or expertise without the need to make them fixed overheads. They increase the speed of response of firms to market conditions. They can encourage the business to develop in different areas at once, thereby spreading the risk by reducing vulnerability to rapid fluctuations in demand.

However, they do depend on firms trusting one another. Combining the names of firms with each other means that clients will associate one with the other. Any damage to the reputation of one could result in damage to the professional image of the other.

This again reflects the importance of common values. For example, if one firm places considerable emphasis on speed of response to clients' demands and the other does not measure up to that, clients will become unhappy with *both*, the first for the recommendation and the other for the "poor" service.

However, joint ventures can work well, enhancing the resource base of both firms, allowing cross-selling to clients, retaining client loyalty and providing a fast and cost-effective solution to meet the ever more technical demands of clients.

However, some professions are not as able as others to use this strategy. Current restrictions of legal professional bodies are resulting in all kinds of complicated accounting! The vexed area of multidiscipline partnerships continues to be debated at length as the professional bodies concerned identify the problems that they would cause. Some multidiscipline partnerships have been formed and are very successful.

6.7.2.4 Internationalisation and strategic alliances

With the market place becoming increasingly global, many organisations are having to cross geographical boundaries. Even when not directly chasing customers, many firms are sourcing suppliers from other countries to reduce operating and labour costs.

Clients need advice therefore across a wide range of jurisdictions. Professional service firms need to respond and be able to service the needs of their clients. E-commerce will further complicate the range of professional knowledge required.

The ability to become international is a reflection, as always, of the attitudes of the owners, the resources available and the potential that the market place offers. Most commercial clients are now operating in a global economy, with many countries involved in the supply chain and in dealing with customers. Some professions are more suited to working internationally than others, depending on the extent of mutual recognition by their professional body as well as the narrowness of the technical nature of their advice.

Strategic alliances offer perhaps a better response for many professional firms. Many formal networks were established in the early 1990s offering the opportunity to cross-refer work. Some resulted in little return for the time investment required to establish them and allow people to get to know each other. Others resulted in amalgamations and takeovers.

Again, the firm should consider the advantage that becoming a member of such an alliance would bring. It should not be seen as an end in itself, but rather as a strategy which supports the firm's aim to, for example, expand its resource base or raise its profile in a specialist area. Too often firms enter into such an arrangement and pay lip service to its involvement in it.

6.8 Putting it into practice

Once the method has been identified, it then has to be implemented. This is the area where most organisations get into difficulty. Many large organisations are very good at analysing the market place, spend a great deal of money (often on consultancy fees) and energy generating options, and then fail to carry any of them through. They may start a change programme or an initiative with a great deal of hype and then face fundamental problems in getting people to respond.

The reasons for this include a failure to check back against the values of the organisation. If this is not done, people will block any attempt to implement the new programme or approach. It is important to show how this option fits within the overall values of the organisation and allows these values to be supported and maintained. If an organisation seems to chase one option after another, people can become very cynical about such initiatives. They know, from experience, that if they do nothing for long enough, management will change direction and try to introduce another option.

One common failure stems from a lack of understanding about the amount of resources (time, energy) or change of skills and attitude required. Both of these should have been identified in the "practicality check".

Another reason can be that, by the time the decision is made, the market place has moved ahead, making the option out of date and/or a competitor has already moved in. Proper scanning at the beginning should have avoided this risk, but with the speed of change and the amount of information available, this may have been missed. This emphasises the importance of going through rather than getting bogged down in the process.

If the market place has moved on, then it is important to look at the impact of that and adjust the options and responses accordingly. Any business plan must be a living document – it must be adaptable and allow the firm to alter its responses. Given the current trends, as previously indicated, it is the businesses that are adaptable and flexible which are gaining market advantage. Given the size and structure of professional partnerships, they should be able to make decisions quickly! Both the shape and the structure of the organisation must support its implementation. These will be considered in more detail in the next segment of the Model for Success.

It will take time to carry through the choice which has been selected. It is important not to lose focus and enthusiasm. It is better to break its implementation down into a number of steps all working towards a common goal, and review progress regularly. Any interim successes and achievements should be promoted to everyone in the organisation to help to keep the momentum going.

CONCLUSIONS

Market awareness and analysis is vital. Firms need to develop ways of managing the amount of information available about current and future trends. They need to appoint market scanners who report regularly to the firm. They need to encourage people to think externally about the firm and its client base – to think creatively and long term. They need to make choices about their futures, and develop options which will support them.

There are many options open to professional firms, which need to be considered and matched against the market trends having the most direct impact on the firm. The investment and energy required to successfully implement any such option is significant and needs to be supported by the whole organisation. Whatever route is chosen, it is important to look at the "people" situation – their skills, knowledge and attitudes as they will have a direct effect on the success of any subsequent implementation.

 ## *KEY ACTION POINTS*

➢ Analyse, prioritise and respond to market trends

➢ Formalise longer term thinking into routine planning sessions

➢ Encourage people to think creatively

➢ Make choices about the future

➢ Focus on the options which will directly benefit the firm

➢ Make sure such options reflect the firm's values and resources

➢ Ensure that high-quality people are retained

➢ Only acquire or join with other firms when the advantages strongly outweigh the disadvantages

➢ Review progress regularly and adjust proactively!

7. Shaping up for Success

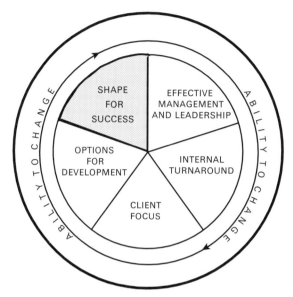

THE MODEL FOR SUCCESS

7.1 Introduction

This segment of the Model for Success concentrates on shaping organisations to meet current demands and future expectations. Structure plays an important role in facilitating the success of professional firms. Their structure tends to be different from other types of organisations who often operate hierarchically, with people having different levels of authority depending on their position. Professional firms traditionally lack such structure and often "confuse" ownership, management and technical operations.

The definition of "structure" includes the formal trading structure offered by partnership as well as by limited company. This chapter considers the allocation of roles and responsibilities between client services, management and support staff, the effect of a "poor" structure and the benefits of a "good" structure. Structure is also important when considering the implementation of strategy. For example, the structure of our firm will be different if we had decided to target high-volume, low-skill client work from that which suits low-volume, high-skill level.

The "shape" of the firm includes the people within the firm. We will therefore consider how to shape and develop new partners, how to deal with succession issues and how to encourage people to "grow". The size of the firm is also relevant. Is there a "good" size? What happens to the shape of the firm as it grows?

7.2 Why is the shape of the firm important?

The shape of an organisation can directly influence the way it currently operates and its future direction or strategy. Academics have often debated whether structure determines strategy or the other way around without coming to a definitive conclusion (e.g. Chandler, 1962). What is agreed is that there must be a close fit between the two. The structure of an organisation is a reflection of its values and resource base and will also determine its potential flexibility. Structure will therefore have a direct effect on what strategy or change of direction can be achieved. As a result, it is important that strategy and structure support each other. There is little point in adopting a team approach to client services if the firm is structured along rigid department lines with poor communications and a separate basis of charging. Clients are unlikely to see this as a seamless service! The shape of the organisation therefore needs to reflect its values and its aims and objectives.

Internally, structure can play an important part in the way firms make decisions. It can also influence the way that they are managed, how they deliver clients' services and how well they respond to change. The "wrong" structure can inhibit effective management, slow down decision making and fragment client delivery.

The structure of an organisation affects how resources are allocated, what reporting mechanisms are needed and the way in which communications and relationships develop. The structure can therefore help or hinder effective working and resource co-ordination. It has a direct effect on the people within the firm in the way that they report and their levels of authority. From the outset of this book, I have indicated that care has to be taken in applying traditional management tools to professionals and their organisations. The importance of this is reflected in this chapter as people's behaviours and values determine how they will behave in certain structures.

For example, where firms have operated in a certain way for a considerable period of time, it becomes difficult to change that way of working and the behaviours associated with it. In addition, if staff turnover is low, and the firm is fairly stagnant, it is even more difficult to change long-established working patterns.

There is also a growing perception amongst professional firms that size matters! This is partly as a result of the increasing influence of the large accountancy firms on the market place, as well as a realisation of the increasing demands on the resource base (mostly as a result of IT). In addition, the structure of an organisation needs to change as it grows. Research (Galbraith and Kazanjian,

1978; Churchill and Lewis, 1983; Smallbone et al., 1990) confirms that the structure that is successful at the start-up stage will not necessarily support subsequent growth. Many a small business has experienced growing pains with the founders having to learn to let go of direct operational control and introduce effective delegation.

The challenge for all professional organisations is therefore to find the appropriate degree of informality to allow change and development with its professionals having as much autonomy as possible whilst, at the same time, ensuring sufficient control to maintain operational effectiveness and consistency in client delivery!

The ultimate aim of the shape of the firm is to ensure that its resources are ulitised to their maximum potential. It is also important to build in flexibility and overcome any resistance to change. As identified earlier, people can become comfortable with the current shape of the organisation and are unwilling to move out of their "comfort zone".

7.3 What happens when the shape is wrong?

Most of us can recognise when the shape of our organisation is "wrong". There seems to be a mismatch between what people say and what they do. For example, some firms will emphasise the quality of what they do, yet pay little attention to measuring that quality. Others will emphasise the role that people play in their success, but do nothing to reward their staff (not just in the financial sense) or recognise their contribution.

When the shape is wrong, the firm seems to be "costly". Resources appear to be wasted, with a great deal of duplication and a lack of co-ordination. Bottlenecks are common, with some people seeming to have too much to do at one and the same time. Communications also appear to be disjointed. People do not seem to know what is happening. Some people get information about the firm, others do not. Decisions (if taken at all!) do not seem to address current needs and/or be based on relevant information. As a result, the overall performance of the firm is poor with opportunities missed. Morale is low with people seeing little point in working hard or making suggestions for improvements. Good people leave and a sense of lassitude sets in. People focus on the negative aspects of the firm rather than the positive.

7.4 Our inherited structure

As discussed before, structure played an early part in the development of modern management techniques. Hickman and Silva (1987) in their review of management history described that, from 1910 until 1935, the structure of organisations was the key focus for business development. A great deal of effort was therefore placed on getting the right structure to deliver business success.

Partnership as a business structure was around long before the establishment of the limited-company option. At the risk of launching into a lecture on the law of partnership and limited companies, it is important to notice that the way most partnerships currently operate is still governed by the 1890 Partnership Act. The Joint Stock Companies Act 1856 made it unlawful for more than twenty persons to continue to trade as a partnership without being registered as a limited company. This continued to be the case until the 1967 Companies Act which, as a result of pressure from professional firms (who at that time were prevented by the rules of their professional bodies from trading as anything other than partnerships), allowed an exemption for solicitors, accountants and stockbrokers. (Further professions were excluded by subsequent statutory instruments.) This reflected the pressure that was beginning to build on professional firms to extend their resource base. This pressure has increased. It is now generally accepted that partnership as a mandatory trading structure is causing difficulties for some professional firms. For example, complicated accounting is resulting from some of the "multidiscipline" options. Some professional firms are hiving off their higher risk work into limited companies. We are now seeing the introduction of a limited-liability partnership option which may offer the opportunity to alter some of the relationships between and among partners as well as with clients. It is too early to say what the take-up will be of that option and what effect it will have on professional firms and their shape.

7.5 The partnership option?

Some professional bodies continue to insist that their members trade as partnerships. Others have for some time accepted alternative trading structures, subject to special rules and regulations, including capital structure and compliance requirements.

Accountants and lawyers often debate the advantages of partnerships over limited-company status with their clients. This includes the flexibility that partnership offers with its range of profit-sharing options and the privacy that it affords with no need to publish accounts. The limited-company option can provide increased protection from liability, and cleaner entry and exit for senior managers. The main drivers for professional firms who have become limited companies seems to have been to reduce people's risk exposure and create the opportunity to "sell on". Those who have opted for this route describe that it offered them the flexibility to grow, to bring in third-party funding and to improve decision making. It also provided an exit route for the owners and/or a better way of valuing the business.

In general terms, most professionals would advise clients against trading as partnerships given the potential exposure to unlimited liability. They would also counsel against a structure where owners interfere in the day-to-day operations, suggesting that the actual running of the business should be left to those with management experience. This advice is reflected in business statistics (Bannock and Daly, 1994; Hicks et al., 1995) which illustrate that, as turnover increases beyond £250,000, the percentage of businesses trading as partnerships decreases.

It seems difficult therefore to understand from the business point of view why organisations would continue to opt for the partnership rather than the limited-company option. This reflects our earlier discussions about the importance of professional values and is one of the questions I often pursue with professional firms. Nearly all reinforce that importance of "partnership" – of the importance of trust and of the direct commitment, both in abilities and resources from the key players. Interestingly, many of those who are considering or have opted for limited-company structure still speak of the importance of professional relationships among the "directors".

7.6 The correct structure

Many professionals ask me to tell them what is the correct structure for their firm, and I have to disappoint them. There is no single correct structure for a professional firm. There is only the correct structure for that particular firm and each firm must work out what that is. This includes both its operational structure and its management structure. The operational structure will depend on the size of the firm, its range of client services, its geographical locations and its style of approach. It can be small and informal, large and formal, regional, networked and/or international.

Its management structure should also be tailored to suit its values. Some firms operate well with one partner in charge – the benevolent dictator who sets the rules and approach adopted by the firm which the other partners are happy to support. Other firms work well with a management team, which implements strategic and operational decisions made by the full partnership, in other words has delegated authority. Some firms successfully appoint a practice manager, who is not "one of their own" but an external professional, brought in because of his or her expertise. Yet others rotate management duties and/or split operational from strategic responsibilities.

Whatever option is chosen, it must support effective communications, manage resource allocation and reporting, and help to co-ordinate and support client services, as well as plans and strategies. It must also be flexible enough to respond to changes in demand and service levels.

There are five essential aspects to whatever structure is selected:

- the firm as a whole must trust the individual(s) concerned;
- everyone must be clear about their levels of authority and responsibility;
- it must provide the whole range of skills;
- it must deliver the resources that the organisation needs;
- it must support consistent and high-quality client delivery; and
- the overall effect must facilitate decision making and implementation.

Finally it must be able to maintain momentum and facilitate change. It must allow the firm to develop.

7.6.1 *Maintaining trust*

Section 3.5.2 has already considered the importance of trust in relation to the management of professionals. Most commercial and not-for-profit entities operate with a board, chief executive and operational managers. People will have defined job roles and responsibilities and failure to implement agreed decisions results in sanctions being imposed. As most professional firms lack this formal structure, it is not possible to manage them in this way. To successfully influence professionals requires that they trust the individuals concerned. Managers need to pay considerable attention to developing that trust (and not underestimate the time that that may take if they are new to the firm).

This also reflects the importance of trust between professionals. Professionals work well with people they trust and will behave in a collegiate way, happy to share their skills and knowledge. However, if no trust exists, the impact of their disruptive behaviour will be felt throughout the organisation. This can be extremely damaging, particularly amongst partners. We have all experienced the effect of partners who do not get on with one another, causing friction and tensions in working relationships!

7.6.2 *Achieving clarity*

Whatever structure is adopted, people must be clear about their level of authority and responsibility. This may be stating the obvious but this area is often overlooked with assumptions made that everyone knows what to do. This may have been the case in the past but, nowadays, firms have become more complicated. More specialist functions have developed. More management and business skills are now required; there is also the need to meet the requirements of external regulations and professional indemnity parameters.

Management committees or managing partners are often appointed without clear lines being drawn between where their responsibility stops and starts. For example, are they acting as agents of the partners or as principals? This fundamental distinction is important as it could allow the partners to disregard their decisions and undermine their authority. The problems caused by appointing non-partner managers have already been highlighted. They may have operational authority but can run into problems when they try to exert it against partners!

This distinction has therefore a direct effect on structure and levels of authority. One of the main aims of clarification of roles and responsibilities is to ensure that administrative details are devolved to as low a level as possible. Professionals have a bad habit of wanting to hold on to details that should not concern them! They should not be involved in debating the installation of new telephone systems or stationery costs, which should be allocated to others to deal with.

Another area that needs to be clarified is when departments are set up. Again, if partners/managers are put in charge of them, are they still answerable to the partnership as a whole for client service delivery or can they adopt procedures of their own which they feel are more suited to the needs of their departments? As before, there is no right answer to this other than to recommend that people need to be clear which route has been selected. If managers have too limited authority, it does call into the question the purpose of their appointment! In general terms, managers should be given as much authority as possible and the support to be able to make it work.

7.6.3 *Providing skills*

Allocating roles and responsibilities within an organisation is all very well but people should not be put into such roles without the skills and support needed to undertake them. Too often, in professional organisations, a decision is taken to restructure with little attention being given to the individuals concerned. It is important that the structure delivers the whole range of skills required – professional, technical, operational and management.

In some cases, the individuals see "management" as a burden they have to bear on behalf of the firm rather than having any real interest and/or ability in it. In other cases, people are promoted to partner/manager without the skills needed to manage people. Professional training places a great deal of emphasis on the technical training and little on business or management skills. Just because people are technically skilled does not necessarily give them people skills! A proper evaluation of any gaps in management skills needs to be carried out, which in turn allows the firm to make informed decisions about future recruitment and training.

Any operational structure must deliver the ability to plan, to motivate, to evaluate performance and client service, to develop strategies and identify market trends, to source resources – both soft (people, knowledge) and hard (capital, equipment). This is a wide range of abilities – financial, marketing, strategic thinking, personnel and human-resource development. Most firms will be unlikely to have all of these. Some will have to be developed and some bought in.

In addition, the structure must deliver the technical skills needed, which may include general professional skills as well as high-level expertise. Senior professionals can help to develop younger professionals or support staff. External consultants can be retained to enhance existing expertise. We identified the importance of developing people within the audit exercises in Chapter 4. People are a major part of the resource base of a professional-services firm.

7.6.4 *Delivering resources*

The structure selected must maximise the resources of the firm in such a way that it delivers what is needed where it is needed. Too often, professional firms invest in expensive IT systems which are only used to a fraction of their potential. In other cases, firms open branch offices and amalgamate with other firms which puts a drain on existing resources, such as personnel support, which is difficult to sustain.

The structure must not become cumbersome and unwieldy. Most professional practices have limited resources and they must be sensibly allocated. There is little point in developing a complicated department structure when the firm does not have the client work to support that degree of specialisation. Many of the larger firms found difficulty with the style of approach when property work declined and people were too narrowly skilled to be able to swap over to other departments. Flexibility is and will continue to be important. As the market requires more adaptability, people will have to be able to join different teams to serve the needs of particular clients. They may also require to work outside the firm in more "joint ventures" with other professional firms. Such teamworking requires a range of skills – both technical and interpersonal.

7.6.5 Supporting quality

The structure must support consistent and high-quality service delivery. This is another area which is often overlooked. In the past, firms often developed a structure which suited them. To cope with the increasing complexity of the work professionals became more specialised. Firms departmentalised and insisted the people fitted into that structure. This resulted in a fragmented approach to client service delivery with different parts of the same firm working in different ways, often charging different rates. Clients were forced to deal with not one but sometimes many people within the firm. This led to a great deal of frustration, with clients often seeing this approach as a reason for charging higher fees and professionals struggling to manage effective internal communications. On occasions, this resulted in the embarrassing situation of the client knowing more about the firm than its own professionals!

Many firms continue to do highly specialised work. Departmental structures can help to support that. If this structure is adopted, it is important that the services the client receives are provided in the same way (e.g. similar styles of reports and documents, similar levels of charging). If at all possible, one invoice should be sent out rather than a series from the individual departments involved. At a bare minimum, the firm must ensure that internally each department makes the other aware of what is happening on each of the files to ensure that the client is not being compromised by a lack of co-ordination. Clients do not appreciate having to explain what they want more than once!

Some firms have now tackled this problem with the appointment of key-client partners. This structure helps the consistency of client delivery as well as providing a feedback loop on the quality of service. Others have developed a client-functional approach, so that, within one department, clients have access to all of the expertise that they will need.

7.6.6 Facilitating implementation

The overall structure must facilitate decision making and its implementation. It must also allow these decisions to be reviewed and adjusted over time. Too often the personalities or behaviours of some of the principals can determine the structure. In one case I experienced, a small firm had introduced an unusually complicated department structure given its size because two of the partners did not speak to each other! Another firm had a strategy and a management committee, both of which reported directly to the full partnership. Each committee was chaired by a very strong personality. It was not clear whether the firm wanted to keep them apart or whether it was determined to water down their influence! These examples illustrate how flexible a structure partnership can be, but neither was designed to facilitate decision making and implementation.

Partnership decision making is notoriously slow and cumbersome. It is important therefore to streamline it as much as possible. Partners' meetings, for example, should discuss higher level issues about the firm and not take up time slowing down decisions that should be delegated to others within the firm. Taking these matters off their agenda alone would accelerate the firm's ability to change!

As discussed earlier, the structure of meetings is important. They should be managed to maximise people's time and input. Partners' meetings should focus on what needs to be decided by the partners! Partners' meetings tend to adopt certain types of "behaviours". Too often people get into bad habits when attending meetings. They tend to arrive with an expectation which reflects what happened in similar meetings in the past. If previous meetings have been laborious and long-winded, they will assume all meetings have to be like that. Similarly, often the most opinionated person polarises opinions and prevents reasoned and balanced discussions. All of this can be avoided with proper planning of agendas and people having access to accurate up-to-date information.

We now need to look at other elements of internal structure, with the caveats already highlighted about regarding communications, resources, co-ordination and adaptability.

7.7 Standardisation

A great deal of emphasis was placed in the 1980s and 1990s on the introduction of standardisation into the ways that organisations were structured. Quality initiatives, such as BS 5750 (now ISO 9000) and Investors in People, sought to ensure consistency of output by setting standards for people to work to. These were taken up and developed by some of the professional bodies, such as Lexcel and the Practice Management Standards of the Law Society and Legal Aid franchise requirements. Others adopted a regulatory approach, seeking to set standards by regular inspections and asking professionals to become "accredited" or licensed specialists. These standards often require formal policies and procedures, and/or planning, review and evaluation processes. They can include internal and external audits and an assessment of the firm's and individuals' performance.

In some cases, as with legal aid, external standards have to be adopted as they are an obligatory part of being able to deliver those services. In other cases, it is for the firm to decide whether to adopt such an approach. There is value to be achieved from the introduction of such standards and/or standardisation as long as the firm identifies the benefits which will be derived from it.

For example, the introduction of formal job descriptions can involve a great deal of effort and discussion. If this allows people to be clear about what is expected of them and reinforces the level of responsibility that they have and it reduces overlaps and streamlines work, then it is worth doing. If the firm is so small that people need to cover for each other on a regular basis and/or client demands change on a daily basis, then there may be little to be gained.

Keeping in mind what benefits will be derived, the firm should identify which parts of the firm or which services provided should be standarised. It needs to distinguish between its internal systems and its external services. Internal systems should be standardised wherever possible. Some client areas will adapt easily and others will not. In some cases, computer software is already available or can be written by individual firms. For example, standard drawings and costings can be developed. Routine house purchases can be readily systemised with key dates and activities identified. One of the overall aims of any standardisation is to improve the efficiency of the firm. It should therefore take away the drudgery of the work, and allow people to concentrate on the higher value or "tailoring" of the service.

Care has to be taken, however, to check whether some areas cannot be so "routinised". Some of the services provided may be so tailored to individual clients that attempts to prescribe a course of action would not be cost effective and dilute the professional's ability to deliver to suit the expectations of individual clients. Clients should not feel that their services have been "standardised". Section 6.6 discussed the importance of differentiation as a useful strategy for most professional service firms. Clients should therefore feel that our service is particular to our firm and their needs. If they feel that what we provide is the same as the firm next door, then they will be more able (and more tempted) to shop around. There is nothing worse than sending a letter or report out to a client which looks as if it has been "churned out". Clients are the first to notice when personal attention to detail is reduced!

This whole area of standardisation is one where people's behaviour will have a direct impact. Few professionals respond well to being asked to standardise what they do, describing that each client situation is different and requires their special judgement of the circumstances. Many an attempt to implement standardisation (indeed routinise anything from fee policies to outstanding balances recovery!) has stumbled because of a lack of acceptance by the firm's professionals. It is essential to manage this resistance to their introduction by, for example, seeking their expertise in devising the standards and, in all cases, referring back to the values of the firm and the benefits that will be achieved.

7.8 Shaping the skill base

Another area, which merits considerable attention, is the need for the firm to shape its skill base not only to support current services but also develop it for the future. Section 4.7 has already identified the importance of increasing delegation to provide a quick and effective solution to improve current levels of profitability and stress levels! This will allow a widening of the skill base – of moving support staff to "para" professionals and allowing the professionals to concentrate on higher level work. We need to develop a picture of the firm – of the skills it needs and the people who will deliver them. We have already identified that most people want to have interesting jobs and take on more responsibility. Firms need to capitalise on this and grow their skill base. Such an approach will support an incremental growth strategy. However, if the firm has opted for accelerated growth, it needs to shape its skill base to support it. This must include both the technical and management skills to achieve this.

It is not always possible to allow everyone to make equity partner and/or as quickly as some people would wish, yet we have established the strategic importance of retaining quality people. Maintaining motivation of good people can be achieved by developing some secondment opportunities. These do not need to be long term, but could be for a limited period or a day a week, working with a key client or other professional firm or contact. Some of the larger firms operate an excellent secondment policy sending young people away to other firms for 1 or 2 years and then bring them back, with increased experience, abilities and confidence as well as an extended contact network. Whilst this option is not available to all firms, creative thinking in this area can pay long-term dividends. For example, it may be possible to ask a client to act as "mentor", or for a young professional to work on a voluntary project for a business-support agency. As already considered, it is important that professionals become more commercial. College lecturers are being seconded to local businesses to learn what employers want from their graduates.

Firms need to develop ways of introducing people to business and management skills. Involving people (not just professionals) in the audit exercises is one way of achieving this. Asking outside experts to deliver in-house training sessions is another. Developing joint ventures with other types of professions also allows this widening of the traditionally limited professional view, as well as transferring, for example, numerate abilities from accountants to written skills from lawyers. A lawyer who understands figures is a much stronger professional as is an accountant who can communicate effectively!

Succession planning is an important aspect of developing the skill base. Because of the personal relationships professionals develop with their clients, such discussions are usually avoided by both the retiring partner and his/her potential successors. The retiring partner is reluctant to hand over clients to people who do not understand them and their particular needs. Younger professionals are therefore unlikely to be able to get to know the clients well enough to understand them! Clients also dislike change. They are at their most "fluid" at this transition stage and should be offered a seamless transfer. Yet, too often, firms take little effort to contact clients other than to send out a routine letter "telling" clients who their new professional is. Many clients comment on this with distaste. They feel that they should be involved in and be comfortable with that selection. It is important to respect this and not simply assume that the client will accept the individual we propose.

It is essential to consider succession issues and plan for the transfer of skills and knowledge which otherwise will be lost. Proper discussion of this in advance of the situation becoming personal is important. Similarly, when a partner or senior professional leaves, the firm should carefully look at the skill base it will need for the future rather than simply assume that it will replace the retiring professional's skills. The market place may have changed and the firm's requirements may be different. For example, it may not be essential to replace a retiring partner with another full partner. The firm may operate more successfully in the future with a partner from another discipline or an externally qualified practice manager. This situation should be seen as an opportunity to shape the firm for the future, rather than being seen as a problem.

7.9 Team working

We have already established that successful organisations are those which have balanced management teams. This means that people are expert in their particular field, that they complement one another and that there is open communications, with sensitive issues discussed.

Many professional clients ask me to help them with team-building exercises. They feel that their organisations are not as effective as they could be and think that improving teamworking will help. In many cases, they will already have a number of informal teams which are working well together. These may include:

- multifunctional client-project teams of professionals, para-professionals and support staff;
- in-house specialist teams such as IT and finance; and/or
- business-development teams of support staff and professionals.

People may be "leading" in one and "following" in another. For example, the IT manager will lead the IT support team, but act as a team member on the business-development team by developing the client database.

The usual problem is not that the organisation is poor at teamworking, but rather the professionals (and the partners in particular) are not behaving as "team players". Most professionals are happy to work in a team situation, as long as they are the leaders!

As discussed in Chapter 4, it is important that the organisation maximises its resources. This can only be achieved if people work well together and co-operate. Most professionals now accept that they need to work in concert with other professionals to allow them to have the resources and people support that they need. It is important to emphasise this aspect with them rather than talk too much about "team building". It may mean the same in practice but professionals like to retain their independence! Many are more comfortable with the phrase "collegiate" which they define as a group of individuals providing mutual support and working towards a common goal. Many of us would argue that this could also be the definition of a team, but the shift in emphasis is important.

There are a number of ways of developing team profiles and a wide range of models available (e.g. Belbin, 1991). These are designed to encourage people to understand each other better – to recognise and respect their differences. Where people have to work closely together, under pressure in an environment where high-quality client services have to be provided, this is important. Otherwise, as stress levels increase, extremes of behaviour can appear. We can all think of some examples of this, many of which outsiders would simply not believe! This is partly the problem, because it is almost accepted in professional firms that people will behave in extreme ways. One solicitor justified this by explaining that "clients choose us because we are strong personalities"! In my opinion, this does not justify people being rude to each other, and arrogant and high-handed with support staff and/or clients. It is always interesting to observe what is "acceptable" behaviour in different organisations. A good indication of this will be what happens in reception areas. People at work copy the behaviour of other people (as in families). For example, if two partners do not speak to each other, their support staff will behave in the same way and will not co-operate or provide cover for each other.

Everyone, including professionals, should be encouraged to work well together. Using team-profiling exercises will allow a better understanding of people's strengths and differences. For example, people who are decisive need to appreciate that other people need time to reflect. People who value analysis need to accept that intuition can be equally important to others. Any team-building exercise should not be done in isolation. People need to practice their new knowledge and understanding in a particular project.

Whilst people need to be able to work well together, this does not mean that there should be no disagreements and debates. We should not seek to eradicate all traces of individuality and personality. Innovative solutions often come about as the result of generating a range of options and some creative tension! People should be encouraged to stretch themselves. This reinforces the importance of trust and respect and of listening. People should be able to give their views and receive a fair hearing.

It is becoming increasingly important for professionals to be able to work in teams outside their organisation. For example, corporate and construction work often involves teams of professionals – accountants and lawyers, surveyors, architects and engineers. As a result, they may have to be able to influence situations where no one professional or individual is in overall charge. This requires interpersonal skills and an understanding of people's behaviours and their dynamics. These can be practised within the firm and then used outside it. If people learn to work well together internally, this will help to reinforce their behaviour pattern externally. It is important to build up their confidence by providing training in areas that need to be reinforced, such as negotiating skills. Increasing their role in and understanding of the firm can also enhance this confidence.

7.10 Does size matter?

There is a growing perception that the size of organisations is important. In the late 1980s and early 1990s, with the world economy under pressure, many of the multinationals downsized, outsourcing many of their non-core and even some of their core functions. Pushed on by the possibility of reaching a global market, many of the largest companies are now merging, seeking ways of increasing their resource base as well as local market knowledge.

Analysis of current professional directories shows a similar trend, with amalgamations a common strategy to increase the geographical reach of firms. Some firms have adopted an "existing product, new market" approach as competition in their local market increased. For some, expansion beyond their professional jurisdictions has served them well.

There is growing pressure on locally based medium-sized firms that traditionally offered a broad range of traditional services, particularly to private clients. Fee rates for this type of work have been forced down. These firms often responded by reducing staff overheads, with the partners doing more of the work themselves, with little time to develop client and business relationships. Yet, one of the current positive trends for them is the growing emphasis placed on regionalisation. Local connections are becoming increasingly important, with these firms well placed to respond.

Many of the larger city firms are continuing to amalgamate, pooling resources and expertise. As long the management and client issues that that option brings are dealt with effectively, these firms should be more able to service the needs of their combined client base and attract new clients. The earlier example of the accountancy firm illustrates the difficulty that a disagreement about values and the future size of the firm can bring. It is important therefore to discuss and agree what size the firm wishes to be and how it wants to get there. If amalgamation is the preferred option, then it is essential that the combined partners of the new firm share the same values for the future firm.

Experience and statistics confirm that size is a factor in the success of professional firms, but it is not the only determinant. On average, the larger firms appear to be more profitable per partner, but it is also possible to be equally profitable when smaller. Overall the larger firms (if properly managed) have the potential to be more successful because of their increased resource base. However, smaller firms can also be extremely profitable and often are more able to respond more quickly to market opportunities/changes.

The overall message is therefore that size is important – but the size of the firm must follow any development option adopted and must reflect the values of the firm and its people. For example, if the firm decides to adopt a niche strategy, its size and structure should reflect this with a core of high-quality professionals providing expert advice in a narrow area or specialism. Other types of work can be referred out to a wider network of firms on a mutual-referral basis. If, however, the firm decides to be broad based serving local clients, its structure should reflect this with a few locally known and respected partners, supported by paraprofessionals doing this typically lower fee type of work. If the firm adopts a high-volume, low-cost approach, it will require tighter operational controls as it will when working with more skilled and autonomous staff.

Any increase in size brings with it a need to look at the structure of the firm, rather than simply continuing in the same way, albeit involving more people. Any business growing in size has a need to restructure – to alter the way that it handles work, perhaps introducing streamlining or batching of processes and/or introducing standardisation. Professional firms are no different and, as they grow, need to develop a new way of operating. Only then will they realise economies of scale, maintaining quality for less costs and using the increased resource base to its maximum potential.

Decreasing in size as an option is rarely talked about until the firm is facing fundamental problems, by which time these discussions can become very personal and divisive. In some firms, its structure is no longer profitable with highly paid people doing lowly paid work. This has to be addressed, with perhaps difficult but necessary discussions taking place before people become polarised. This reflects the importance of the earlier audit and analysis exercises (Table 4.2) which encourage people to debate options on the basis of facts rather than subjectively.

7.11 Share of profits structure

The next area of structure that we need to consider is profit-share, which is always one area where the professionals show their creative skills! There appear to be no limit to the possible options when it comes to working out partners' share of profits, ranging from firms where the partners go away every year for a day and thrash out last year's share to firms where one partner makes the decision and then tells the others. Other firms, because of the restrictions imposed by their professional bodies, have set up complicated cross-charging arrangements to ensure a fair share of profits to those who have contributed to them. Other firms have a fixed structure where people work towards equity shares over an agreed passage of time, regardless of ability or contribution.

I cannot provide examples of what is a "good-profit share structure" and what is not. What works for one firm will not work for others. There are as many options as there are firms. As with other areas discussed, whatever model is chosen must work for *that* firm and reflect its values. If, for example, the firm places considerable emphasis on teamworking, then the split should reflect that. If the firm wants to grow "their own" future partners, then partners who are prepared to spend time and energy coaching and mentoring others should be rewarded for that. Most models will contain some element of subjective judgement. The people who make that judgement must have the trust and respect of other people.

It is also possible to come up with a variety of other options. These can include setting up a company which is then able to pay out "shares of profits" to support staff, setting up joint ventures with associates (who can be partnerships or limited companies), and, following the American model, have individual professionals becoming "limited companies" in their own right.

7.12 Moving through the partnership structure

More often than not there is no formal career path within professional partnerships. In some professions, it is usual for people to become a partner by the time that they are in their late twenties. In others, they may have to wait until their mid-thirties. Historically, people were expected to make few moves between firms and certainly remain within professional practice if they were to make partner. Too many moves had the appearance of "being unstable"!

As developed in Section 6.7.1, the traditional carrot of partnership no longer assures that young professionals will stay and work hard with the same firm through their early careers on the expectation of becoming a partner in that firm. Not only do they move between firms more readily to gain experience and/or widen their CV, they are not so attracted by the risks attached to unlimited liability unless they see the rewards are there for them. Even firms with a quality reputation and client base find it difficult to attract and keep good young professionals. Are there structures that can help to support this?

Again, it is important to look at the values of young professionals and what motivates them. Few are motivated solely by money, most will respond to being allowed to learn, to tackle quality work and work with more experienced seniors. Any structure that supports these factors will help to keep and energise them.

Most firms cannot make everyone a partner just through passage of time. There has to be some selection process – formal or informal. We discussed in Section 3.5.1.3 that developing a profile of what makes a good partner in the firm is a valuable exercise. Most partner profiles contain the same core elements:

- the ability to work with clients, contacts, staff and colleagues;
- technical and professional skills, both general and specialised;
- basic professionalism and ethics;
- business-awareness skills, including finance and management; and
- the ability to deliver results.

In addition, there is a growing need to develop professionals with the ability to think creatively and with vision.

Not everyone will be naturally good at all of these but, with training, everyone can improve. If the firm develops such a profile of a partner, it allows younger professionals to work towards achieving that shape. It also helps to retain their interest in and commitment to the firm as well as providing an objective framework for the partnership to take decisions about who "makes partner".

It follows that the next stage down should also be formalised (i.e. associate partner, senior manager, department head). It is useful to follow this structuring through the whole firm – office managers, supervisors, para-professionals and support staff. This ensures that people are clear about their roles and responsibilities as well as providing a structure for people to progress through. Some kind of formal appraisal process is also important as it helps to ensure the objectivity of assessment of people's performance and contribution to the firm. This is another area where this attempt at structuring could clash with the preferred behaviour of professionals. Professionals feel that only they can be the judge of their competence and, as a result, do not behave well when being asked to accept the introduction of a formal appraisal process. Great care must be taken to ensure that the policies and standards imposed "fit" the firm. Any procedures introduced must be tailored to the values of the firm and its style of management.

7.13 Strategic structures

It is important to look at our external structures; in other words, those relationships which we have with other organisations. The essential for any external structure developed by the firm is that it provides access to resources and market information. To achieve this, some firms have joined formal networks or associations (e.g. within the construction sector). Some of these work well by increasing the resource base of the firm, as well as offering the potential for direct referrals of work and/or clients. Other firms have adopted a less formal approach, referring work out to other professionals if the services sought by the client are outside their area of expertise and/or not profitable for them to undertake. Some multidiscipline associations have been formed with clients being offered a package of support. Other ways of extending the resource base include membership of professional bodies, trade associations and teaching institutions. These can also provide the "external awareness" which is vitally important in today's changing market place.

Too often partners work in isolation from each other, building their personal networks and connections. What is of equal importance is that the firm develops some mechanism for capturing information – about the resources themselves and their availability and about external indicators. These mechanisms can include monthly business-development reports, which include details of contacts made and/or an effective (up-to-date and accessible!) database.

7.14 Knowledge management

This leads on to current theories about knowledge management. It is now accepted practice that the effective management of knowledge will provide competitive advantage for organisations in the future (Drucker, 1992; Amidon, 1997; Edvinsson and Malone, 1997; Rajan et al., 1999). Successful organisations are those which are client focused and are able to respond to clients' demands. As clients become more sophisticated, firms need to develop innovative ways to respond – to add value to their services. This requires the firm to be aware of and to capture the knowledge that exists within it.

The shape of the organisation must therefore facilitate its development. This shape must include the culture, again reflecting the importance of the establishment of values, trust and respect. People will be unwilling to share their skills and knowledge unless the environment is open and supportive. Innovation requires the ability to adapt and respond, to solve problems and try out different options.

As work practices change and people work more flexibly, it is important to provide ways to allow them to access external information. Technology offers ways of achieving this. As indicated earlier, GPs are being offered a dedicated television channel to help them keep up to date with developments in their field. More and more sophisticated databases are available offering access to property values and statistics, recent legislation, court and tribunal decisions.

In addition, the firm needs to develop ways of capturing its internal knowledge – to devise systems to identify people's expertise and develop ways of sharing it (von Krogh et al. (eds) 1998 offer a number of interesting examples of these). Too often our knowledge is carried around in our heads. All organisations need to introduce ways of turning what is implicit into explicit. Some of this can be achieved through in-house training sessions and/or discussions. Some of this will be affected by the layout of our organisations, with departments on different floors and/or buildings experiencing problems of sharing and communicating. All will be influenced by the degree of openness and trust which exists. People will be reluctant to give away their expertise and their "power" if they feel that they are being taken advantage of! This reinforces the need for organisations to develop ways of rewarding people who share with and develop others.

Formal processes of capturing and sharing knowledge can include appointing mentors, collating internal profiles of people, developing intranets and/or standardising routine information-update reports. It is also important that these processes encourage the development of knowledge – to encourage people to constantly stretch and learn new skills.

CONCLUSIONS

The shape of the firm is important and must match the values of the organisation and the approach it takes to client service delivery. "Shape" includes both the structure of the firm and its people, communications and workflow. A close fit is needed between the shape of the firm and its development options to achieve organisational effectiveness.

Any structure selected must be adapted as the firm develops. It must provide enough formality to effectively manage the business as well as allowing people to maintain as much autonomy as possible. The ultimate aim is to achieve flexibility and maximise the leverage of the resources of the firm at all times as the demands of the firm change and adjust.

Partnership offers a range of options and styles. The strength of partnership as a trading structure rests on the existence of trust, an essential element of effective management. Some firms are moving towards a limited-company option. Any alterations to the shape of the firm need to maintain that trust. If that is achieved, people will be more likely to respond to and work to support the firm.

KEY ACTION POINTS

> Make sure that the shape of the organisation reflects its values

> Recognise the signs of having a poor structure

> Consider options other than partnership

> Remember there is no template for an effective structure so be wary of adopting a shape which suits other organisations

> Make sure that whatever structure is adopted is effective and provides all of the resources that the organisation needs, now and in the future

> Any standardisation must improve service delivery and efficiency

> Shape the skills base for current – and future – needs

> Be careful of too much emphasis on teamwork

> Watch that the size is effective

> Remember that, as the organisation grows, its shape and structure will need to change

> Match share of profits and reward systems to our values

> Make sure that any external structures add value

> Manage the knowledge of the organisation.

8. Working in the Commercial and Not-for-profit Sectors

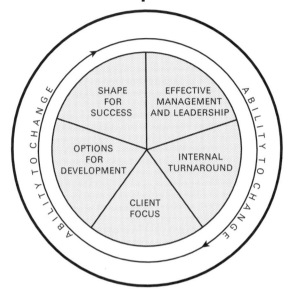

THE MODEL FOR SUCCESS

8.1 Introduction

At the outset of this book, we started from the premiss that professionals need help. This applies equally to professionals working in the commercial and not-for-profit sectors. They are experiencing the same pressures to change as those working in professional firms. However, they are likely to have additional problems as they seek ways of balancing the demands of their organisations with their own and their professional values.

This book is also aimed at people who have responsibility for managing professionals in all types of situations. These managers need help as they try to integrate these people into their structure and service delivery.

Previous chapters have discussed individual segments of the Model for Success. It has been tested against and is equally relevant to the needs of all professionals. Working through the segments will also deliver the complete circle of success for them. Some additional aspects will now be developed to put the Model into the context of professionals working in commercial and not-for-profit sectors.

8.2 Setting the scene

Not all professionals work in private practice. Some work in commercial organisations, serving "internal clients" such as senior management and other departments. This can result in problems associated with balancing the demands of their organisation with their professional responsibilities. Professionals may be promoted into management positions, without any training in this area. They may be managed by people not necessarily from the same background as themselves, which can result in difficulties of understanding. At one level, there may be a lack of a shared language with problems over the jargon being used. At a higher level, there may be the potential for clashes between professional and commercial opinions.

Many professionals work in the not-for-profit sector – in hospitals, schools, colleges and universities, in local and central government, in public-sector support and in a wide range of charities and voluntary organisations. They may have to cope with a number of influences on them and the services that they deliver. Their funding may come from a number of sources. They may use volunteers or work closely with people from other organisations. The ultimate end-users of the services they provide may not pay directly for them. All of this affects they way that they work.

More and more professionals are working as subcontractors or self-employed consultants. This relationship, although similar to that of professional and client, can also create problems of agreed expectations. For example, client organisations may consider that the work they have commissioned is sensitive and confidential, and are disturbed to find that their consultant is also retained by one of their competitors.

Regardless of whether they work within the public or private sector, the challenges facing professionals remain the same. All professionals:

- place great emphasis on the importance of their values;
- debate the increasing complexity of their work;
- discuss the impact of technology on what they do;
- are concerned about the growing emphasis on commercial decisions;
- worry about the loss of their professionalism; and
- talk about increasing pressure and stress levels.

In turn, managers in those sectors often describe that their professionals appear to:

- play "devil's advocate";
- block and delay decisions;
- be not "on their side";
- debate the theory rather than the practice;
- be distant and not committed;
- have a conditioned mindset; and
- not understand commercial reality!

The external market place has a direct impact on everyone as the line between the public and private sector is becoming blurred. For example, we have seen the increasing privatisation of our public utilities and telecommunications. Joint partnerships are becoming more common, with the development of PFI and similar initiatives. Contracting out on an operational basis is also on the increase. As a result, both private and public sectors may have to work in harmony, with private restaurants opening in museums, and schools using outside caterers.

The commercial market place is becoming more and more competitive. This is forcing internal reviews of work practices, reductions in overheads and improvements in product and service delivery. Professionals working in these types of organisations are being asked to become "more commercial" and to respond faster to the needs of their internal clients. They have to prove their worth by working with other departments to add value to the end product.

Professionals working in the not-for-profit sector are also being made responsible for budgets and meeting performance standards. Their organisations can often place considerable emphasis on the demands of funders and external influencers, whilst the professionals continue to emphasise client/patient service.

The shape of all organisations is altering. With changes in work practices, with the development of IT, with the need to reduce fixed overheads and to become more flexible, many large organisations are downsizing. They are becoming smaller, working with core staff and a range of subcontractors. We are seeing the development of "virtual organisations" (Handy, 1995), where people work at a distance from each other, coming together only for key projects. Job security is no longer taken for granted, even in the public sector, where many people are now on fixed-term contracts. All of this has a direct impact on how people behave and can be managed. Everyone is being asked to respond to and manage change. Creating an acceptance of change has become one of the most critical challenges for managers in every sector.

As we have discussed in Section 2.4, organisations more often fail through a lack of effective management than as a result of any external market pressures. Successful organisations are those which are lean, focused, intelligent in their use of IT, close to their customers and responsive to change. People need to be flexible, working in teams which adapt to meet client demands. They need to share their experience and knowledge and find innovative solutions to product and service delivery. Status within the team is not based on job title but on expertise.

The original research behind the Model was based on professional firms. It has been tested on and applied to all professionals, regardless of their type of organisation. Each element holds true:

- (segment 1) professionals will only be managed by people who they trust and respect;
- (segment 2) all organisations need to analyse their resource base and maximise its potential;
- (segment 3) all organisations need to be "client focused", matching their levels of service to the demands placed upon them;

- (segment 4) all organisations need to identify their options for future success; and
- (segment 5) all organisations need to adapt their shape to support these.

As indicated earlier the Model is designed to deliver an acceptance of change and the ability to achieve it.

8.3 Effective management and leadership

The definition of effective management and leadership contained in Chapter 3 continues to be valid. As we discovered, organisations that are well managed are more likely to succeed. This is true of all sectors. Drucker (1989) argues that not-for-profit organisations in fact need effective management more because they lack the "discipline of the bottom line!"

Unlike most professional firms, different people may carry out leadership and management in commercial and not-for-profit organisations, which can cause problems of communication and consistency. People can become confused when leaders say one thing and managers another. This reinforces the need to discuss the values of the organisation and develop an agreed "frame of reference". Once this has been established, both managers and leaders have a framework to refer back to when potential differences arise.

The range of stakeholders who need to be involved in these value discussions is often much wider than with professional firms. These may include:

- third-party funders;
- shareholders and members;
- customers and clients;
- staff and managers;
- board and committee members;
- volunteers and subcontractors;
- direct and indirect partners;
- regulatory organisations; and
- other influencers within their network.

This wide range can result in conflicting values. For example, the funders may want to emphasise research projects, whilst staff are focused on service delivery. The organisation will need to find a way of satisfying both. Working through the values exercises in Chapter 3 (Tables 3.1 and 3.2) will help to identify these and agree an umbrella under which people are prepared to co-operate.

If professionals feel that their advice is not heeded and that their values are being challenged, they will not stay with the organisation. Balancing all four value boxes continues to be valid and highlights the external and internal strains that can arise if that is not achieved. Many large organisations will have formally developed their values into mission or vision statements. These should be mapped into the matrix and then checked against those of the individual and professional bodies. Some organisations use these values as a powerful part of their recruitment and induction process, as people can quickly identify whether they match their own. However, it is important that these values are then delivered by the organisation!

It is important to resolve any tensions that exist between being perceived as being commercial as well as professional. This is particularly the case where professionals are currently working in the public sector and/or have moved from the public to the private sector. Many feel that too much emphasis is being placed on finance and budgets at the expense of client services. These issues need to be discussed and resolved. They may stem from a misunderstanding of the interpretation of what these words mean. They may be based on a real dichotomy between what is feasible and what is not. In either event, they need to be debated and clarified. If a problem exists in practice, then action must be taken. If not, professionals will work round the system to either frustrate or dilute any reduction in their professionalism.

As discussed in Section 4.5, it is important to include relevant and accurate information about the financial position of the organisation. This may also require training in basic finance and business skills as this will not have been included in most professional training. However, professionals learn quickly and will soon challenge figures which are irrelevant and based on false assumptions. Management must be confident of their own understanding and rationale!

Leadership and management skills continue to be those which facilitate decision making, strong chairing skills, including the ability to listen and influence. The ability to inspire the trust and respect of professionals is often based on previous track record and reputation, which can be more difficult to achieve in larger, multidiscipline organisations. It is important to make full use of the networks of professionals to allow them to find out about their leaders' and managers' past history and performance. Other than that, professionals will reserve judgement until they see the calibre of a new leader or manager in action.

Developing this recognition also depends on open communications and trusting people with confidential information. Leaders and managers should seek the advice and support of their professionals at an early stage, challenging their intellect to help to develop practical options to resolve problems. If professionals appreciate the difficulties and contribute to their solutions, they are much more likely to be willing to implement them.

Senior managers should not underestimate the power that their professionals will have in influencing behaviour throughout the organisation. At best, they will be mischievous if they feel they are not part of the decision-making process. At worst, they will be directly confrontational and will challenge and undermine authority. Their behaviour may have an influence on and be copied by other staff. In addition, it is important not only to identify but also to position other key influencers. If their commitment is required to effect change or implement options, this should be built into any action planning.

The outline business plan (Table 3.3) highlights the various elements which should be included. Many public-sector organisations need to follow a template business plan, which can have the effect of limiting their thinking and analysis. It is important that this does not happen and that the future and its trends are identified. The use of key-performance measures in all cases should include external benchmarks. Funding implications can place considerable emphasis on efficient use of resources, rather than the effectiveness of the organisation. It is important that performance measures are extended beyond finance and numbers to include some qualitative evaluation, which helps to illustrate to professionals that the organisation places value on other aspects of its service delivery.

Larger organisations often develop standards, policies and procedures. It is essential that these are consistent with the agreed values of the organisation, as too often there is an apparent conflict between the two. For example, there is little point in emphasising the importance of teamwork and finding innovative solutions if the organisation's approach to budgets encourages rivalry between departments and no risk taking! Some organisations have adopted quality standards as a way of ensuring consistency of product or service delivery. As discussed before, professionals use their judgement to tailor their service to the needs of individual clients. This approach causes friction with the introduction of such quality standards, and can create tensions between managers and professionals.

As discussed in Chapter 3, professionals will only be managed and led by people that they trust and respect. They do not respond well to being policed and told to adopt certain ways of working. They will be the judge of their competence and decide what individual client situations require. Many hospital managers will confirm this! It is essential therefore to give them as much independence as possible, as well as reinforcing that these standards support high-quality client services. It is also important to involve professionals in the initiation and development of the standards themselves.

8.4 Turning the organisation around

Commercial organisations will find all of the elements of the audit exercise in Table 4.2 directly relevant. It is important to have open and informed discussions around workloads and performance. Given the degree and rate of change being experienced by all sectors, it is likely that alterations will be required to the way that people work, the type of work that they do and the range of products and services delivered.

A SWOT analysis (Tilles, 1968) is a useful starting point and should involve all the stakeholders if at all possible. Different stakeholders will have different perceptions of the organisation, which need to be built in and addressed. The weighting given to each of the elements of the audit should be adjusted to meet the style of the organisation. People will always play an important part. As we know, professionals can be powerful influencers on the behaviour of others. They can be dynamic and caring. They can also be disruptive!

Care should always be taken when attempting to introduce any people-management procedures. Professionals will resist any attempt for anyone other than themselves to judge their competence. In addition, they must also comply with their professional body's requirements for continuing professional development, regardless of any funding support available from their employing organisation. Because of this a number of alternative models have been developed. For example, a separate committee of professionals may take responsibility for review and evaluation of the professional input into service delivery, and any resultant training or support.

Finance, budgets and cash flow are relevant nowadays to all sectors. In not-for-profit organisations, values can be powerful drivers for everyone with the perception that all are "committed to the cause". This can cause an overemphasis on values at the expense of some more rational and/or long-term choices. Access to reliable data is always important to allow objective discussion of options, rather than subjective opinions. In some public-sector organisations, the funding structure causes complicated accounting and performance measures. Again, it is important to ensure that the data is accurate, as professionals will take issue with any assumptions that have been made.

Pricing may not be directly relevant for not-for-profit situations, but service levels will be. Again, professionals will have to be educated to accept that clients are the judges of quality. Administration and systems may be provided by external suppliers rather than within direct control. If that is the case, then they should be audited as "suppliers" to check effectiveness and value for money.

When analysing the client base it is important to consider the service and product mix. The matrix developed by the Boston Consulting Group (Henderson, 1970) can be adjusted to suit the public sector by consideration of those services which attract funding and/or political support. In some situations, it will be possible to use surpluses generated from the Cash Cows to support the other three. In other cases, because of the requirements of external funders and their audits, it will not. It may not always be possible to drop Dogs as there may be services which have to be supplied regardless of their future potential. If that is the case, it is important to identify and try to manage them as effectively as possible and/or outsource them. Again, this approach may clash with the values of the organisation and its professionals, who may be committed to providing a service to the community regardless of its cost.

Competitor analysis may appear to be more important for commercial organisations, but the not-for-profit sector should also be careful to look at this aspect carefully. Increasingly it is seeing both direct and indirect competition, as the private sector moves in to challenge many of its monopoly positions. Not only does such analysis allow organisations to position themselves within their market place, it also provides valuable information about quality, service levels and trends.

All organisations should identify areas which will provide direct returns and quickly. This will allow people to see the value of the exercise and, incrementally, reduce resistance to change. As people become more aware of the strengths and weaknesses of the organisation as a whole when they are asked for their input and support, they become better informed and more able to contribute.

8.5 Client focus

Few organisations would argue today against having a customer or client focus. Most sectors are under pressure to continually adjust to the demands of the market place. The situation described in Chapter 5 is similar in both the commercial and not-for-profit sector.

Competition in the private sector has caused a change of emphasis; for example, banks and building societies are shifting from money management to "selling services". There has also been a marked shift in recent years in many aspects of public services, who now provide customer helplines and proactive advice. This can put people under pressure if they have to work within resource and time constraints. The management of stress is now an integral part of health-and-safety requirements. It was not an accident that the first reported case of a successful claim for stress at work came from the public sector. All of this requires careful management and support.

Clients are the judges of the quality of the service. The sample questions offered in Table 5.1 can be adapted to suit commercial or not-for-profit customers and clients. Establishing clients' expectations upfront is also important, as it may not always be possible to "delight" everyone. Many public-sector organisations have to deal with people who have been forced by their circumstances to ask for their help. It is not always possible to provide that help. Realistic expectations should be tackled and established at the outset.

Clients may have to deal with a number of professionals within the organisation. It is important therefore that people do not "pass the buck", leaving it for another department or someone further down the line to tell clients that their expectations cannot be delivered. Good data management is important as this saves time and irritation for all parties. Again, working with people on the basis of trust and respect will allow both sides to achieve satisfactory outcomes.

Effective communications continue to be important, with training provided to help to deal with "difficult people". Dealing with complaints is important in all sectors and is often a source of valuable feedback on service levels and clients' expectations.

Professionals working in large organisations often provide services to other departments (i.e. they have internal clients). These should be dealt with in the same way as external clients. In many cases, tensions appear as professionals are brought in at a late stage and/or are asked to rubber-stamp a decision. As indicated in earlier chapters, professionals do not respond well to that style of approach. It is important to "educate" internal clients by providing them with summaries of the key elements that they need to be aware of and also, as far as possible, to integrate professionals into operational matters. This helps them influence decisions at an early stage. It also educates them in the issues of management and allows them to prove their worth to other members of the organisation.

The public sector often has a number of "clients" who have to be kept satisfied. The people who pay for the services are often not the end-users. This can cause internal problems with people either unclear about the ultimate customer or serving one at the expense of the other. It can also cause external problems where the public and/or other organisations feel that they have a right to express opinions about access to or levels of service. It is important that these issues are discussed and clarified as otherwise internal tensions can be created. All of this causes pressure on staff and managers.

8.5.1 Time management

The management of time is crucial in any sector. Most organisations are leaner than in the past, with everyone being asked to do more with less. People must therefore be encouraged and supported to use their time effectively. The techniques provided in Chapter 5 are important and their use should be introduced.

Delegation by professionals should also be encouraged wherever possible. Not only does it make good commercial sense to have work carried out at the most efficient level, it also allows people to develop and to take on more responsibility. Large organisations may experience problems with this if job roles/descriptions are narrow and formal. If that is the case, this should be addressed as successful organisations are those which can adapt. This can be difficult to achieve quickly and may involve discussions with employee representatives. It is important to be open about the reasons behind any change, rather than talk about "multi-skilling" and "empowerment". People tend to view jargon with suspicion in the absence of hard facts and direct face-to-face communications from senior management.

People acquire habits and behaviours in any organisation. Outsiders are often quick to notice bad practices which are being taken for granted. This is particularly the case where staff are long established or have limited experience of working elsewhere.

Most people complain of spending too much time in meetings. Some organisations adopt a habit of meeting, regardless of whether that is the best mechanism. It is usually possible in most sectors to make considerable savings on people's time just by carrying out a check on the number of meetings held, their duration and outcomes. This will identify a number which are unnecessary, too long, badly structured and ineffective. Reducing these will not only free up people's time; it will also reduce their stress levels!

8.6 Developing options

As discussed in Chapter 6, awareness of the market place is important for all organisations. The public sector is as affected by changes in society, technology and the economy as is the private sector. Trends are important indicators of current and future demands for client services. Market research is used by both sectors and provides useful information about service levels and customers' perceptions.

Porter's 5 Forces (1980) encourages a holistic view of the pressures being placed on all organisations. For example, the threat of substitute products from the private sector is shifting the demands placed on the public sector. It is foreseeable, for example, that hospital trusts will be left with less profitable patient care as the private sector attracts the "upper end" of services. The public sector is becoming increasingly competitive. Consider the growth in the numbers of universities and training providers, all competing for the same adult learners.

It is important to be able to think creatively and long term. Changes of direction and choices may have to be made. In every case, organisations will have to check these against their values and current and future resources.

The importance of values in the not-for-profit and voluntary sector has already been highlighted as important drivers of people's commitment. They may care passionately about the organisation and what it stands for, and are unhappy about changing the way that they serve their clients. However, there may well be pressure to change, stemming from alterations in legislation and/or indirect competition for funding. In general terms, most have had to become more commercially aware, with the result that management training may be required for their board members, senior managers and professionals.

The development options for commercial organisations are similar to those available to professional firms. Some are adopting a niche strategy, concentrating their efforts on a key client base. Both the commercial and not-for-profit sector are increasingly using amalgamations and joint ventures to expand their resource base and expertise. There have been a number of high profile mergers in recent years, particularly in the financial-services sector. Hospitals have joined together to achieve critical mass catchment areas, often based on the premiss of achieving economies of scale. Such a route must bring long-term benefits. The importance of matching values continues to be essential.

There can often be conflict between the aspirations of all of the stakeholders. Professionals may argue that they need to adhere to the requirement of their professional bodies, funders may look for performance related to use of resources, and clients may demand services tailored to their needs. Staff may be committed to the philosophy underpinning the organisation, which they feel is out of line with current resource levels. Any long-term development option must identify these conflicts and introduce ways of reducing them. It is unlikely to be possible to meet everyone's expectations, and priority choices may need to be made, otherwise implementation will be frustrated. This reinforces the need for open communication and informed debate.

8.7 The shape of the organisation

As indicated in Chapter 7, the shape of organisations is important. Child (1984) identified a number of problems caused by structural deficiencies. These included low morale and motivation, poor decision making, lack of co-ordination, rising costs and a limited ability to change. Organisations from both the public and private sector will recognise these.

Most large organisations adopt a formal structure. Even with the current emphasis on downsizing, this is likely to be more clearly defined than is the case with most professional partnerships. Ownership and management are usually separated with leaders and managers splitting strategic and operational issues. It is usually difficult to change the shape of large organisations, where people will have defined job descriptions, gradings and pay structures. Many mergers have spent considerable time dealing with problems related to company cars and their equivalent in the new structure! Within the public sector, many people work in a stratified and/or department structure, which limits flexibility and the organisation's ability to develop teams and share skills. This means that change is difficult and slow to achieve. It is important to keep everyone as informed and committed as possible, as well as developing ways of rewarding performance. Successful examples include public-sector organisations who have integrated staff and "manuals", and developed "self-managing" teams.

However, as we discussed in Section 7.2, the shape of any organisation must support its choices and future direction. Many of the large financial institutions restructured drastically in the 1990s, removing layers of middle managers. Many manufacturing companies are reducing their dependence on semi-skilled workers by outsourcing and retraining staff to handle quality checks and product design. Another influence on the shape of organisations is the growing importance of developing partnerships with other organisations. As always, such a relationship must be founded on trust and mutual values. If an organisation has a reputation that it cannot be trusted, then it will find it difficult to attract other organisations to work in partnership with!

The elements of an effective structure must include that managers must be trusted and inspire respect, and that everyone is clear about what level of authority they have. It must provide the whole range of technical and management skills, including financial expertise, market awareness and people development. It must be able to source and deliver the resources needed, it must support high-quality product or service delivery and it must facilitate decision making and implementation. In addition, in larger organisations, it must make conscious attempts to develop open and clear communications. Care should be taken when emphasising the importance of teamworking, as professionals may interpret that to mean that they will be the leaders!

Professionals who work as subcontractors or external consultants are also part of the shape of the organisation. It is important to carefully consider their role and relationship with other people. At a minimum, they should be made aware of any policies and procedures that affect them and what standards are expected of them. If appropriate, they should be encouraged to share expertise with others within the organisation, so as to reduce dependency on them.

Good knowledge management is becoming increasingly important for all organisations as it can result in faster response times, reduce costs, improve profitability and stimulate innovation. However, to achieve this, managers have to be able to develop a culture where people share skills and expertise. This can be difficult in the current climate of mergers, downsizing and lack of long-term job security. Managers and leaders have to be able to respond to that challenge. They need to persuade people that they are prepared to invest in them and their future. That future may not necessarily lie with that organisation, but whilst working with them, people will be supported, allowed to learn, given quality work and experience. They should also be given recognition for what they have achieved for themselves and the organisation.

This shift in culture is fundamental and can be exciting to some people and terrifying for others! Hammer (1996) provides an excellent summary of the "move from worker to professional" which illustrates many of these cultural issues.

CONCLUSIONS

There are many similarities between professionals working in professional partnerships and those working in the commercial and not-for-profit sectors. All of the segments of the Model are relevant to professionals and those responsible for their management. Professionals behave in the same way in all types of organisations and continue to reflect the influence of their values, their independence and their professional bodies.

It is important to manage professionals by establishing their trust and respect. They should be involved in discussions about the values of the organisation, and should be encouraged to debate any dichotomy between being both commercial and professional. The impact of their behaviour and its influence on other people is considerable.

Professionals should be given as much independence as possible. If the organisation wishes them to adopt policies and procedures, then it should involve them in their creation. Any financial information should be as accurate as possible, as professionals will challenge any inconsistencies. If client services have to be adjusted to meet budget requirements, professionals should be given autonomy to do so within agreed parameters. Both the clients and organisation will be damaged if it attempts to drop the quality of service below an acceptable professional level.

The shape of all organisations is changing with more emphasis being placed on both internal and external partnerships. As always, such a relationship has to be founded on trust and respect of one another. Effective knowledge creation and management is becoming increasingly important for all sectors.

 ## *KEY ACTION POINTS*

≫ Ensure that managers understand their professionals

≫ Do not underestimate the influence professionals have on people's behaviours

≫ Develop a "frame of reference" to help the identification and delivery of values

➢ Ensure that professionals are aware of the credentials of their leaders and managers

➢ Provide management training for professionals

➢ Involve professionals in the development of policies and procedures

➢ Make sure that financial and management information is not based on false assumptions

➢ Check the client's definition of a quality service

➢ Watch the effectiveness of meetings and what they achieve

➢ Provide external professionals with clear guidelines of what is expected of them

➢ Develop partnerships (internally and externally) through the establishment of trust and respect

➢ Develop ways of sharing knowledge and expertise.

9. Achieving Success

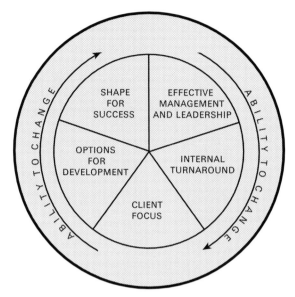

THE MODEL FOR SUCCESS

9.1 Introduction

Most of us feel under pressure at the moment because of the pace of change around us. Many of us are working hard, struggling to keep the important elements of our lives and work in balance. As a result, there is a risk that we become overwhelmed and depressed about the future of professionals and their organisations.

Instead, we should accept that change creates positive opportunities for us to grow and develop. Professionals traditionally work well under pressure and have the potential to respond powerfully and creatively. This book provides examples of firms that have responded in this way – that have managed and continue to manage change. As a result, they are successful. They have good internal relationships, challenging and stretching work, strong client loyalty, good profit levels and a healthy resource base to support future growth.

Professionals and their firms may not be easy to manage, but this does not mean that we should abandon any attempt to do so. We have to be careful not to overemphasise the commercial aspects of our organisations. Professional firms provide important and valuable services to a wide range of clients who need their help. Professionals, by their very nature, care about these services and are committed to their delivery. Their values are the main drivers behind their energy and professionalism.

9.2 Effecting change

All organisations need to be able to change. This allows them to respond to the market place and the opportunities it presents. Clients expect us to service their needs. We need to be able to adapt to these demands and, as a result, constantly acquire new skills and knowledge. Achieving change allows people to grow and to take on more responsibility. As a result, we are able to increase our resource base which will provide the potential for the future success of both our organisations and ourselves.

However, people fear change. As a result, they respond by refusing to work together, blaming each other for problems and generating disinformation. To overcome this, we need to be aware of these responses and be able to support people through their concerns. Regardless of the sector or the size of the organisation, to successfully manage change requires a number of key elements. These include:

● open and honest communications;
● the establishment of trust and respect;
● mutual understanding;
● accurate information about strengths and weaknesses;
● a willingness to learn and a culture which supports it; and
● the development of new skills and ways of working.

Throughout the book, we have identified and developed the tools and techniques to allow us to achieve this.

Most organisations are facing similar trends and pressures. These include the impact of new technology on traditional ways of working, increasing direct and indirect competition, and a shortage of resources, particularly skilled staff. As a result, we have to become leaner and fitter, more able to adapt and maintain close links with our clients.

Within professional organisations, our main competitive advantage comes from our people. They are an integral part of the services we deliver. As a result, it is important to support people in coping with change and develop them to:

● work co-operatively;
● have self-awareness, confidence and be independent;
● be aware of their skill base rather than their job title;
● have good communications and facilitation skills;
● be able to influence people without having direct authority over them;
● take responsibility for themselves and their work;
● be willing to learn and allow other people to learn; and
● become comfortable with change.

Over and above that, they need the technical skills and knowledge to deliver high-quality professional services, and be able to work in partnership with people.

9.3 Developing partnerships

We started with a debate about the usefulness of partnership as a trading structure and have come full circle. The structure of partnership allows flexibility and the potential to be adaptable and client responsive. It focuses powerfully on the people element of business relationships. The essence of any partnership is the establishment and maintenance of trust. We have seen that successful organisations are those which developed open and honest communications based on hard data, good rapport and understanding, and the ability to adapt and respond. It is not a coincidence that these are the same core elements which help people cope with change.

They are equally as relevant to client relationships as they are to internal relationships. To work well with our clients, we have to inspire their trust and respect and, at the same time, be able to trust and respect them. Good client relationships are based on clear and agreed expectations of what each side will achieve, coupled with the ability to work together and adjust to changes in circumstances.

External partnerships are also important. As the market place expands and clients demand more and more of us, we need to extend our reach and resource base. As a result, we have to develop relationships with other professions, organisations and networks. By associating with them, we trust them with our image and reputation, providing them with confidential information about our expertise and ourselves. Again, both sides need to be open and honest and agree mutual benefits.

9.4 Examples of success

Throughout the book, we have identified firms that have achieved success. They come from all professional sectors, and include large regional organisations and small local practices. The features which they have in common include that they:

- have written business plans and statement of values;
- ensure that people work co-operatively and flexibly;
- set high targets and benchmark themselves against other organisations;
- use financial performance as a measure of success rather than a driver;
- have achieved improvements in internal efficiency through the integration of technology in the way that they work;
- invest and continue to invest in technology and training;
- have a clear client focus and have changed the way they work and the shape of their firm to respond to clients' needs;
- meet with clients regularly to check their perception of service delivery and establish what is important to them;
- have established themselves in a niche position and continue to build their reputation by providing leading-edge services;
- do not allow themselves to get distracted chasing every opportunity;

- have developed ways of working in partnership with other organisations and are happy to share their expertise as well as learn from other people; and
- continue to adjust their structure and skill base to cope with future changes in demands.

As a result, architect practices have shifted their internal emphasis from the production of drawings and costings to design. Solicitor firms are managing high volumes of work *and* producing a quality service. Surveyors are providing project-management skills rather than narrow technical functions. Some multi-discipline structures offer both short- and long-term flexibility, with firms able to adapt their service delivery to fluctuating client and market demands.

9.5 The Model for Success in practice

The Model offers the potential for success. It provides a number of practical tools and techniques to put it into practice and, as a result, develop the ability to change. Each organisation must start at the segment of the Model which reflects its current stage of development.

As a result, some firms will need to concentrate on segments 1 and 2 – on management, leadership and turning the firm around. This will allow them to establish trust and respect, open and honest communications and stabilise their resource base by effecting some crucial changes. Key actions at this stage may include:

- investing in management by recruiting external skills;
- eradicating a blame culture;
- sorting out fundamental cash-flow problems;
- establishing what work is profitable and shifting emphasis towards it;
- identifying key clients and nurturing them; and/or
- changing the way people work as a result of investing in technology.

Other firms will concentrate on segment 3 and their client focus. This will allow them to develop strong working relationships with their clients, and be more comfortable about selling themselves and their firms. Key actions for them may include:

- educating everyone about costs and fees;
- providing training in listening and questioning skills;
- improving everyone's time management;
- establishing an effective client complaints procedure; and/or
- developing partnership arrangements with key clients or connections.

The most sophisticated of all organisations will concentrate on segments 4 and 5. As a result, they will spend time looking ahead to develop exciting choices about their future direction. This will allow their more daring professionals to stretch themselves and use their creativity and energy in a positive way. As a result, key actions may include:

- completing a comprehensive analysis of the market place and its potential;
- developing a unique niche position;
- attracting and retaining high-quality professionals;
- developing innovative structures by sourcing external partnerships; and/or
- developing creative profit-sharing arrangements.

The Model is designed to allow us to be successful and to stay successful. This requires that we develop the ability to change and keep changing. Professionals and their managers working in other types of organisations will also find examples in each segment of the Model to help them cope with and manage change.

It is not a coincidence that segment 5 lies next to segment 1. This reinforces the continuing nature of change and the importance of shaping the firm not just for its current needs, but also for the future. The shape of the firm must provide the management and leadership skills to support its future development. It must reinforce the continued existence of trust and respect, and of open and honest communications.

The Model also emphasises the importance of a tight fit between each of the segments. Organisations and people have limited energy and resources. If the segments do not fit well together, it becomes much more difficult to turn the wheel. People may be unclear about what is expected of them, resources may be inadequate or misaligned, departments may have differing priorities, and effort will be wasted and dissipated. The Model requires that all of the segments fit closely together and support each other. As a result, the Model creates energy and dynamism, driving the organisation forward.

Conclusions

Success is possible. Pressure to change should be seen as a powerful opportunity to expand the skill and resource base. People need to be supported and managed through their natural reluctance to alter their established ways of working. They need to work with people they trust and respect; in other words, they need to work in partnership.

Professionals and their organisations have the opportunity of a powerful future. Current trends indicate that knowledge will become increasingly important in the market place of the future, along with the ability to sort, prioritise and apply it. Professionals have this ability and will be key players in the management of knowledge. As the pace of change accelerates and the complexity of life increases, they will be able to use their intellect to develop innovative solutions to client situations. As a result, they will be able to shape their own success.

KEY ACTION POINTS

> ➢ Manage change and support people

> ➢ Develop internal and external partnerships

> ➢ Work through the Model to achieve success

> ➢ Ensure a tight fit between all the segments

> ➢ Generate energy and drive, and

> ➢ Look forward to the future!

10. Diagnostic Questions

These questions are designed to allow professionals and their organisations to identify how successful they are in implementing each segment of the Model for Success. Underpinning all of the questions, we need to keep asking ourselves: Are we able to change and keep changing?

Segment 1 – Chapter 3 Effective Management and Leadership

Effective management

Are people committed to improving the management of the firm?

Have we the skills and resources to achieve it?

Leadership

Have we talked about our values?

Have we resolved any conflict between being professional and being "commercial"?

Have we agreed the fundamental values of the firm?

Do we have a clear frame of reference to make decisions against?

Are people comfortable with talking about money?

Do people trust and respect each other?

Do we openly communicate with people?

Planning

Do we have a clear and agreed plan for this year and the next 2 to 3 years?

Are we clear about our priorities?

Do we have accurate, up-to-date information about the firm?

Have we defined what we mean by "success"?

Do we use performance indicators (quantitative and qualitative) to measure that success?

Implement

Can we implement that plan?

Organise

Do we have all of the resources we need at the moment?

Can we access the resources we will need in the future?

Control

Is the firm working effectively?

Are people clear about the standards we expect of them?

Have we formalised as much of our internal processes as we can?

Are policies and procedures followed as a matter of routine?

Adjust and respond

Can we respond to changes in demand for services?

Overall

Do people talk about job satisfaction, get excited about client projects?

Can we think of examples of people sharing expertise, working co-operatively and supporting each other?

Can we give examples of recent achievements by the firm?

Segment 2 – Chapter 4 Turnaround to best practice

Open and informed discussions

Are we able to have open and informed discussions about issues affecting the firm?

Strengths and weaknesses

Do we know the firm's strengths and weaknesses?

Have we checked them with other people?

People

Do we have an accurate picture of our current skill levels and expertise?

Do we know our future skills needs?

Do we have a picture of the skills of a "good partner"/associate partner and other roles in the firm?

Are our "people" processes, such as performance reviews, adding value?

Finance

Do we accurately know our current financial position?

Are our monthly management accounts clear and succinct?

Do people use and rely on them to make decisions?

Pricing and service levels

Are we feeing at the right level?

Do we know what work is profitable?

Have we analysed our use of time?

Are our levels of work-in-progress manageable?

Are fees being paid promptly?

Suppliers

Are we purchasing supplies effectively?

Administration and Systems

Are we maximising the use of office space/systems/IT/equipment?

Clients

Are we aware of our sources of new business?

Do we know why clients choose our firm?

Do we know which clients/type of work is profitable?

Do we know what services our clients value?

Do we have a balanced spread of services?

Are we developing new services to support future profitability?

Quality

Are we checking how clients evaluate the quality of our services?

Are we externally benchmarking the quality of our service?

Competitors

How well are we performing against our direct competitors?

First steps to success

Do we have a clear short-term plan of priorities and actions we need to take?

Have we the resources to undertake them?

Are we regularly reviewing our progress?

Delegation

Is work being done at the correct level?

Are there "production" bottlenecks in the firm?

Do we support people to take on more responsibility?

Have we developed ways of making sure that people do what they enjoy?

Are meetings effective?

Overall

Can we give examples of changing the way people work which have had a positive effect on overall efficiency?

Can we give examples of people taking on more responsibility which have improved overall performance?

Can we give examples of our investment in IT, producing direct benefits for the firm?

Segment 3 – Chapter 5 Improving our Client Focus

Client loyalty

Do we ask clients what they think of us?

Do we attract and retain quality clients?

Do we know what services they will want in the future?

Do we stay in touch with all of our clients?

Do we have regular meetings with key clients?

Delighting the customer

Do we know what services our clients want from the firm?

Do we establish mutual trust and respect with them?

Do we tailor our services to suit their needs?

Do we really listen to our clients?

Developing a good client relationship

Do we send out clear terms of engagement?

Do we agree outcomes, timescales and costs with clients upfront?

Are our people good at talking about costs and able to give accurate fee quotes?

Do we get rid of the clients we do not want?

Managing our time

Are our people accessible?

Do people overcommit?

Are people managing their time effectively?

Does the firm reward effectiveness rather than people who "appear" to be busy?

Complaints

Are complaints monitored and responded to?

Are people supported when client problems develop?

Selling ourselves and our firm

Are people comfortable with selling the firm?

Are we actively developing the firm's profile and image?

Are we constantly developing key contacts and clients?

Are we making the most of our selling opportunities?

Overall

Do we see examples within the firm of good working practices?

Can we give examples of clients making positive recommendations about the firm to other people?

Can we give examples of recent "partnerships" with clients?

Segment 4 – Chapter 6 Options for Development

Knowledge of the market place

Do we regularly analyse the external market place?

Do people describe current trends in a positive way?

Do people look forward to the future?

Strategic thinking

Do people think creatively?

Do we encourage people to think longer term?

Does the firm take time away from work to think?

What is the market place telling us?

Are we able to describe the key external pressures on the firm?

Does the firm know what priority to give to each one?

Have we developed specific actions to cope with them?

What choices do we have?

Have we considered and evaluated a range of options?

Have we made a choice about our future direction?

Did we check this choice against our values and what was practicable?

How are we going to get there?

Have we established how that choice will be implemented?

Have we put steps in place to achieve it?

Can we give examples of joint ventures which are working well?

Overall

Can we give examples of the firm responding to changes in the market place in a positive way?

Can we give an example of a creative solution we have developed to enhance the firm's services?

Segment 5 – Chapter 7 Shaping up for Success

Why is shape important?

Is our shape flexible enough to allow us to respond to clients' demands?

Does it make the best use of our resources?

Will it support our future direction?

Is our shape wrong?

Are communications poor?

Is co-ordination difficult?

Is morale low?

Do we have the correct structure?

Are we able to maintain trust?

Are people clear about their level of responsibility and authority?

Does our structure provide the skills we need?

Does it allow us to make the best use of our resources?

Is it flexible enough to allow us to respond to changes in workloads?

Does it support consistent and high-quality client services?

Do we emphasise the importance of good internal communications about client projects?

Does it allow decisions to be made and implemented quickly?

Does it allow people to respond quickly?

Have we standardised routine elements of client services to allow people to concentrate on "adding value"?

Shaping the skill base

Are we constantly upgrading the skill base of the firm?

Do we discuss succession issues?

Do we encourage people to progress?

Size

Are we the right size?

Have we changed our structure to match our current size?

Share of profits

Does our share-of-profits structure match our values?

Strategic structures

Do we regularly use external people and resources to help the firm grow and develop?

Knowledge management

Are we managing our knowledge effectively?

Are people able to access the firm's information and expertise easily?

Overall

Can we give examples of where teamworking has achieved direct benefits for the firm?

Are people able to describe a career path and/or opportunities to develop within the firm?

References

Adler, H. (1994) *NLP – The New Art and Science of Getting What You Want*, Judy Piatkus (Publishers) Limited, London.

Amidon, D. M. (1997) *Innovation Strategy in the Knowledge Economy*, Butterworth-Heinemann, Boston.

Ansoff, I. (1968) *Corporate Strategy*, Harmondsworth.

Bannock, G. and Daly, M. (1994) (eds) *Small Business Statistics*, Paul Chapman Publishing.

Belbin, R. M. (1991) *Management Teams: Why They Succeed or Fail*, Heinemann Professional Publishing, Oxford.

Bennis, W. (1998) *Managing People is like Herding Cats*, Kogan Page, London.

Birley, S. and Niktari, N. (1995) *The Failure of Owner-Managed Businesses – The Diagnosis of Accountants and Bankers*, Institute of Chartered Accountants in England and Wales.

Boyle, R. D. and Desai, H. B. (1991) Turnaround strategies for small firms, *Journal of Small Business Management* **29**(3).

Burns, P. and Harrison, J. (1996) Growth, in *Small Business and Entrepreneurships*, Burns, P. and Dewhurst (eds), J. Macmillan Business, London.

Carson, D., Cromie, S., McGowan, P. and Hill, J. (1995) *Marketing and Enterpreneurship in SMEs – An Innovative Approach*, Prentice Hall, Hemel Hempstead.

Chandler, A. D. (1962) *Strategy and Structure – Chapters in the History of the Industrial Enterprise*, The MIT Press, Cambridge, MA.

Child, J. (1984) *Organisation – A Guide to Problems and Practice*, Harper and Row.

Churchill, N. C. and Lewis, V. L. (1983) Growing concerns – The five stages of business growth, *Harvard Business Review* May/June, 30–50.

Cooper, R. and Sawaf, A. (1998) *Executive EQ: Emotional Intelligence in Business*, Orion Business Books, London.

Davis Hill and La Forge (1985) The Marketing/Small Enterprise Paradox: A Research Agenda, *International Small Business Journal* **3**(3).

De Bono, E. (1992) *Serious Creativity*, Harper Collins, New York.

Department of Trade and Industry (1998) *Our Competitive Future: Building the Knowledge Driven Economy*, The Stationery Office, London, Command Paper 4176.

Department of Trade and Industry (1999) *Our Competitive Future: UK Competitiveness Indicators 1999*, DTI Publication 4248/8k/12/99NP.URN 99/1249.

Department of Trade and Industry (2000) *Regional Competitiveness Indicators*, DTI, London.

Drucker, P. F. (1989) What businesses can learn from non profits, *Harvard Business Review* July/August, 88–93.

Drucker, P. F. (1992) The new society of organisation, Harvard Business Review September/October, 95–104.

Edvinsson, L. and Malone, M. S. (1997) *Intellectual Capital*, Judy Piatkus (Publishers) Limited, London.

Galbraith, J. R. and Kazanjian, R. K. (1978) *Strategy Implementation – Structure Systems and Process*, West Publishing Co.

Gibb, A. (1984) Developing the role and capability of the small business advisor, *Leadership and Organisational Development Journal* 5(2).

Greiner, L. E. (1972) Evolution and Revolution as Organisations Grow, *Harvard Business Review* July/August, 37–46.

Hammer, M. (1996) *Beyond Re-engineering*, Harper Collins, London.

Handy, C. (1995) Trust and the virtual organisation, Harvard Business Review May/June, 40–50.

Henderson, B. D. (1970) *The Product Portfolio*, Boston Consulting Group, Boston, MA.

Hickman, G. R. and Silva, M. A. (1987) *The Future 500 – Creating Tomorrow's Organisations Today*, Unwin Hyman, London.

Hicks, A., Drury, R. and Smallcombe, J. (1995) *Alternative Company Structures for Small Businesses*, ACCA, London.

Hofer and Schendel (1978) *West Series of Strategic Management*, referred to in Galbraith, J. R. and Kazanjian, R. K. (1978) *Strategy Implementation – Structure Systems and Process*, West Publishing Co.

Johnson, G. and Scholes, K. (1997) *Exploring Corporate Strategy: Text and Cases*, Prentice Hall, Hemel Hempstead.

KPMG Corporate Finance (1994) *Where Does Scottish Business Get Its Corporate Services?*, Joint Report with Scottish Financial Executive and Scottish Enterprise.

Kaplan, R. S. and Norton, D. P. (1996) *The Balanced Scorecard – Translating Strategy into Action*, Harvard Business School Press, Boston.

MacMillan, I. C., Kulow, D. M. and Khoylian, R. (1989) Venture capitalists' involvement in their investments: Extent and performance, *Journal of Business Venturing* 4(1).

Miller, D. and Friesen, P. H. (1984) A longitudinal study of the corporate life cycle, *Management Science* 30, 1,161–1,183.

Milne, T. and Thompson, M. (1986) Patterns of successful start-ups, in *Readings in Small Business*, Faulkner et al. (eds), Gower.

Mintzberg, H. (1979) *The Structuring of Organisations – A Synthesis of the Research*, Prentice Hall, Englewood Cliffs, New Jersey.

Nicou, M., Ribbing, C. and Ading, E. (1994) *Sell Your Knowledge – The Professional's Guide to Winning More Business*, Kogan Page, London.

Otterburn, A. (1998a) *Profitability and Financial Management*, Law Society, London.

Otterburn, A. (1998b) *Cash Flow and Improved Financial Management*, Law Society, London.

Peters, T. and Waterman, R. H. (1982) *In Search of Excellence*, Harper Collins, London.

Peters, T. and Austin, N. (1985) *A Passion for Excellence*, Harper Collins, London.

Porter, M. E. (1980) *Competitive Strategy: Techniques for Analysing Industries and Competition*, Free Press, New York.

Porter, M. (1985) *Competitive Advantage*, Free Press, New York.

Rajan, A., Lank, E. and Chapple, K. (1999) *Knowledge Creation and Exchange*, Focus Central, London.

Richardson, B. and Richardson, R. (1989) *Business Planning – An Approach to Strategic Management*, Pitman, London.

Robertson, M. R. (1994) *Contemporary Strategic Issues Workbook*, Leeds Metropolitan University, Leeds.

Robinson, R. B. and Pearce, J. A. (1984) Research thrusts in small business strategic planning, *Academy of Management Review* January, 128.

Royal Society of Arts (1998) *Redefining Work*, Royal Society of Arts, London.

Royal Society of Arts (1999) Opening minds, *RSA Journal* 2/4.

Senge, P. M. (1990) *The Fifth Discipline: The Art and Practice of the Learning Organisation*, Doubleday.

Siegel, R. Siegel, F. and Macmillan, I. C. (1993) Characteristics distinguishing high growth ventures, *Journal of Business Venturing* 8(2).

Slatter, S. (1984) *Corporate Recovery: A Guide to Turnaround Management*, Penguin.

Smallbone, D., Leigh, R. and North, D. (1990) High growth performance in small and medium sized manufacturing enterprises, in *Towards the 21st Century – The Challenges for the Small Business*, Robertson, M., Chell, E. and Mason, C., ICA Print Associates, Manchester.

Stacey, R. D. (1993) *Strategic Management and Organisational Dynamics*, Pitman, London.

Susskind, R. (1996/1998) *The Future of Law – Facing the Challenges of Information Technology*, Clarendon Press, Oxford.

Thompson, J. L. (1997) *Strategic Management – Awareness and Change*, International Thompson Business Press, London.

Tilles, S. (1968) Making strategy explicit, in *Business Strategy*, Ansoff, I. (ed.), Penguin.

Torstendahl, R. and Burrage, M. (eds) (1990) Promotion and strategies of knowledge based groups, in *The Formation of the Professions – Knowledge State and Strategy*, Sage Publications, London.

Turok (1988) Which firms grow?, paper presented to *Small Business National Research and Policy Conference*, published in Davis and Gibbs (eds) (1991) *Recent Research into Entrepreneurship*, Avebury, Aldershot.

van Maanan, J. and Birley, S. R. (1984) Occupational communities: Culture and control in organisations, in *Research in Organisational Behaviour*, Vol. 6, Staw, B. and Cummings, L. (eds), JAI Press, Greenwich, CT.

von Krogh, G., Ross, J. and Kleine, D. (1998) *Knowing in Firms – Understanding, Managing and Measuring Knowledge*, Sage Publications, London.

Wack, P. (1985) Scenarios: Uncharted waters ahead, *Harvard Business Review* September/October, 73–89.

Waterworth, D. (1987) *Marketing for the Small Business*, Macmillan.

Wheelen, T. L. and Hunger, J. D. (1989) *Strategic Management and Business Policy* Addison Wesley, Reading, Massachusetts.

WINtech (1990) referred to in Advisory Council on Science and Technology (1990) *The Enterprise Challenge: Overcoming Barriers to Growth in Small Firms*, HMSO.

World Future Society (1999) *Outlook 2000, The Futurist* 33(10).

Index

National Training awards 62
NLP (Neuro Linguistic Programming)
  84–85
New Scientist 95
Newsletters, client 78
Nicou M, Ribbing C & Ading E 81
Not–for–profit organisations 137–150
  background 138–140
  Boston Consulting Group 143
  client base 143
  client focus 143–145
  communications 144
  competitor analysis 143
  development options 145–146
  finance 143
  growth options 145–146
  knowledge management 147–148
  leadership 140–142
  management 140–142
  marketplace 16, 138, 145
  options, development 145–146
  Porter's 5 Forces 145
  pricing 143
  professionals 138–139, 147
  shape 146–148
  structure 146–147
  subcontractors 147
  SWOT 142
  time management 145
  turnaround 142–143

Organic growth, see Growth – natural
Options
  commercial sector 145–146
  development 25, 93–116,
  growth 106
  not–for–profit sector 145–146
Otterburn A 58

Partner
  development 132
  profile 55, 132
  progression 132–133
  rewards 132
  succession planning 127–128
Partnership
  change 153
  developing 153
  share of profits 131
  structure 132–133
  trading structure 6

  working with clients 78
Partnership Act 1890 120
People management 45, 53–57, 68–69
Performance indicators 43–44
Performance reviews 55–57
Peters T & Waterman R H 14,75
Peters T & Austin N 14, 75
Planning 16, 40–44, 64–66
  accurate information 43–44
  business plan see table 3.3 41
  clients management 86–87
  critical success factors 43–44
  marketplace 97
  process 42–43
  succession 127–128
  trend analysis 94
Porter M E 14, 97, 101, 106, 108, 145
Porter's 5 Forces 101–105
  clients 101–102
  commercial sector 145
  competitors 103
  not–for–profit sector 145
  quality staff 102
  substitute products 104
  suppliers 102–103
Practice Management Standards 125
Pressure 1–3
Pricing 58–60
  commercial sector 143
  not–for–profit sector 143
Professional
  versus commercial 4
Professionals
  behaviour 6
  client focus 73–92
  commercial sector 138–139, 147
  consumerism 21
  definition 18
  future trends 22–23
  how clients choose 81
  impact of technology 20–21
  not–for–profit sector 138–139, 147
  trends 20, 22–23
Professional firms
  differences from other organisations 14
  marketplace 19–20,
  successful 5–6
  structure 6
  MDPs (multi discipline partnerships) 6
Profits, share of 131